Academic Encounters

2nd Edition

READING
___
WRITING

Bernard Seal
Series Editor: Bernard Seal

CAMBRIDGE
UNIVERSITY PRESS

CAMBRIDGE
UNIVERSITY PRESS

University Printing House, Cambridge CB2 8BS, United Kingdom

One Liberty Plaza, 20th Floor, New York, NY 10006, USA

477 Williamstown Road, Port Melbourne, VIC 3207, Australia

4843/24, 2nd Floor, Ansari Road, Daryaganj, Delhi – 110002, India

79 Anson Road, #06–04/06, Singapore 079906

Cambridge University Press is part of the University of Cambridge.

It furthers the University's mission by disseminating knowledge in the pursuit of education, learning and research at the highest international levels of excellence.

www.cambridge.org
Information on this title: www.cambridge.org/9781107602977

First published 1996
Second edition 2012
20 19 18 17 16 15 14 13 12 11 10

Printed in Malaysia by Vivar Printing

A catalogue record for this publication is available from the British Library

Library of Congress Cataloging in Publication Data

Seal, Bernard.
[Reading, study skills, and writing]
Academic encounters, human behavior, level 4 : reading and writing / Bernard Seal. — 2nd ed.
p. cm. — (Academic encounters. Human behavior)
Includes index.
ISBN 978-1-107-60297-7 (Student's book)
1. English language—Textbooks for foreign speakers. 2. Human behavior--Problems, exercises, etc.
3. English language—Rhetoric. 4. Readers--Human behavior. 5. Academic writing. 6. College readers. I. Title.

PE1128.S37 2012
428.2'4—dc23

2012012506

ISBN 978-1-107-60297-7 Student's Book
ISBN 978-1-107-60300-4 Teacher's Manual

Additional resources for this publication at www.cambridge.org/academicencounters

Cambridge University Press has no responsibility for the persistence or accuracy of URLs for external or third-party internet websites referred to in this publication, and does not guarantee that any content on such websites is, or will remain, accurate or appropriate. Information regarding prices, travel timetables, and other factual information given in this work is correct at the time of first printing but Cambridge University Press does not guarantee the accuracy of such information thereafter.

Art direction, book design, and photo research: Integra
Layout services: Integra

Table of Contents

Scope and sequence

Unit 1: Mind, Body, and Health • 1

	Content	Ⓡ Reading Skills	Ⓦ Writing Skills
Chapter 1 The Influence of Mind over Body page 4	**Reading 1** What Is Stress? **Reading 2** Coping with Stress **Reading 3** Stress and Illness	Thinking about the topic Predicting Reading for main ideas Thinking about what you already know Scanning Thinking critically	Parallel sentence structure Hedging

Chapter 2
 	
Lifestyle and Health
 	
page 29
	Reading 1
	Heart Disease
	
	Reading 2
	Smoking
	
	Reading 3
	Healthful Behavior
		Personalizing the topic
		Skimming
		Thinking about the topic
		Increasing reading speed
		Comprehension after speed
		  reading
		Scanning
		Thinking critically
		Scientific terms
		Reading for main ideas
			Comparing
			Understanding paragraph
			  structure

Unit 2: Development Through Life • 55

	Content	Ⓡ Reading Skills	Ⓦ Writing Skills
Chapter 3 The Teen Years page 58	**Reading 1** Defining Adolescence **Reading 2** Physical Change in Adolescence **Reading 3** Cognitive and Social Development in Adolescence	Personalizing the topic Previewing art Reading for main ideas Previewing art and graphics Skimming Reading for details Thinking critically	Understanding paragraph structure Understanding text structure Hedging Gerunds as subjects
Chapter 4 Adulthood page 82	**Reading 1** Early Adulthood **Reading 2** Middle Adulthood **Reading 3** Late Adulthood	Personalizing the topic Previewing art and graphics Reading actively Thinking about the topic Applying what you have read Examining graphics Increasing reading speed Comprehension after speed reading	Using data from a graphic Journal writing Paragraph topics Paragraph main ideas Supporting main ideas Paraphrasing

V Vocabulary Skills	A Academic Success Skills	Learning Outcomes
Guessing meaning from context Dealing with unknown words The Academic Word List	Highlighting Preparing for a test Answering multiple-choice questions Taking notes using arrows	Write an essay on health risk factors
Describing change Describing experimental results	Answering true/false questions Preparing for a short-answer test Writing short answers to test questions	

V Vocabulary Skills	A Academic Success Skills	Learning Outcomes
Word families Synonyms	Definition answers on tests The SQ3R System (Part 1) Taking notes in the margins The SQ3R System (Part 2)	Write an essay comparing and contrasting two adjacent periods of life
Collocations Guessing meaning from context Describing change	Synthesizing Group projects	

V Vocabulary Skills	A Academic Success Skills	Learning Outcomes
Words related to the topic Guessing meaning from context Ways of looking	Outlining practice Highlighting Taking notes Exploring key concepts Writing short answers to test questions	Produce a handbook that will help someone who is not a member of your culture understand how your culture uses body language
Word families Collocations	Making a chart Answering a short-answer test question Exploring key concepts Synthesizing	

V Vocabulary Skills	A Academic Success Skills	Learning Outcomes
Using new words in context Words related to the topic Collocations	Outlining practice Exploring key concepts	Write an essay in which you analyze one or two of your personal relationships
Prepositions Words related to the topic Similar and different	Mnemonics Preparing for a test Taking notes	

Academic Encounters: Preparing Students for Academic Coursework

The Series

Academic Encounters is a sustained content-based series for English language learners preparing to study college-level subject matter in English. The goal of the series is to expose students to the types of texts and tasks that they will encounter in their academic coursework and provide them with the skills to be successful when that encounter occurs.

Academic Content

At each level in the series, there are two thematically paired books. One is an academic reading and writing skills book, in which students encounter readings that are based on authentic academic texts. In this book, students are given the skills to understand texts and respond to them in writing. The reading and writing book is paired with an academic listening and speaking skills book, in which students encounter interview and lecture material specially prepared by experts in their field. In this book, students learn how to take notes from a lecture, participate in discussions, and prepare short oral presentations.

Flexibility

The books at each level may be used as stand-alone reading and writing books or listening and speaking books. They may also be used together to create a complete four-skills course. This is made possible because the content of each book at each level is very closely related. Each unit and chapter, for example, has the same title and deals with similar content, so that teachers can easily focus on different skills, but the similar content, as they toggle from one book to the other. Additionally, if the books are taught together, when students are presented with the culminating unit writing or speaking assignment, they will have a rich and varied supply of reading and lecture material to draw on.

A Sustained Content Approach

A sustained content approach teaches language through the study of subject matter from one or two related academic content areas. This approach simulates the experience of university courses and better prepares students for academic study.

Students benefit from a sustained content approach

Real-world academic language and skills
Students learn how to understand and use academic language because they are studying actual academic content.

An authentic, intensive experience
By immersing students in the language of a single academic discipline, sustained content helps prepare them for the rigor of later coursework.

Natural recycling of language
Because a sustained content course focuses on a particular academic discipline, concepts and language naturally recur. As students progress through the course, their ability to work with authentic language improves dramatically.

Knowledge of common academic content
When students work with content from the most popular university courses, they gain real knowledge of these academic disciplines. This helps them to be more successful when they move on to later coursework.

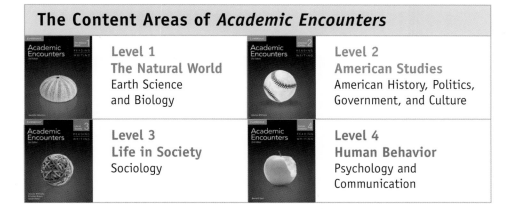

The Content Areas of *Academic Encounters*

Level 1
The Natural World
Earth Science and Biology

Level 2
American Studies
American History, Politics, Government, and Culture

Level 3
Life in Society
Sociology

Level 4
Human Behavior
Psychology and Communication

Academic Skills

Academic Encounters teaches skills in four main areas. A set of icons highlights which skills are practiced in each exercise.

R Reading Skills

The reading skills tasks are designed to help students develop strategies before reading, while reading, and after reading.

W Writing Skills

Students learn how to notice and analyze written texts, develop critical writing skills, and apply these in longer writing tasks. These skills and tasks were carefully selected to prepare students for university study.

V Vocabulary Development

Vocabulary learning is an essential part of improving one's ability to read an academic text. Tasks throughout the books focus on particular sets of vocabulary that are important for reading in a specific subject area as well as vocabulary from the Academic Word List.

A Academic Success

Besides learning how to read, write, and build their language proficiency, students also have to learn other skills that are particularly important in academic settings. These include skills such as learning how to prepare for a content test, answering certain types of test questions, taking notes, and working in study groups.

Learning to Read
Academic Content

PREPARING TO READ

1 Skimming ®

Quickly skim "Facial Communication." In which sections can you read the following ideas? Write *1*, *2*, or *3* on the line depending on whether the idea is in Section 1, 2, or 3 of the reading.

Section 1: Facial Expressions
Section 2: Facial Management
Section 3: Facial Feedback

___ **a.** Some facial expressions are easier to interpret than others.
___ **b.** People adjust their facial expressions to be socially acceptable.
___ **c.** An expression on someone's face can affect how they feel.
___ **d.** People may alter their facial expressions in different interpersonal situations.
___ **e.** Context can affect how people interpret a facial expression.

2 Words related to the topic ⓥ

> Sometimes in a reading you will encounter topic-related words that all belong to the same group. You may need to learn this group of words and the differences between them.

A This text refers to a number of emotional states that the face can express. Work with a partner. Share the meanings of the words you know and find out the meanings of any words that neither of you know.

happiness _____	disgust _____
surprise _____	contempt _____
fear _____	interest _____
anger _____	bewilderment _____
sadness _____	determination _____

B Define the states from Activity A using the following language:

X is an emotional state that you feel when *Y* occurs.

C Write the adjective forms of these words on the lines in Activity A. Use a dictionary to help you if necessary.

Pre-reading is a crucial step in the reading process. *Academic Encounters* teaches important skills to **help students succeed** when preparing to read university textbooks.

The readings come from **university textbooks**, so students improve their ability to **read authentic academic materials.**

Reading 2

SPATIAL MESSAGES

Space is an especially important factor in interpersonal communication, although we seldom think about it. Edward T. Hall, who pioneered the study of spatial communication, called this area **proxemics**. We can examine this broad area by looking at proxemic distances.

5   Four proxemic distances correspond closely to the major types of relationships. They are intimate, personal, social, and public distances.

proxemics
the study of how people manage the space between themselves and other people

Intimate distance

In intimate distance, ranging from the close phase of actual touching to the far phase of 6 to 18 inches, the presence of the other individual is unmistakable. Each individual experiences the sound, smell, and
10   feel of the other's breath. The close phase is used for lovemaking and wrestling, for comforting and protecting. In the close phase, the muscles and the skin communicate, while actual words play a minor role. The far phase allows people to touch each other by extending their hands. The individuals are so close
15   that this distance is not considered proper for strangers in public. Because of the feeling of inappropriateness and discomfort (at least for some Americans), the eyes seldom meet but remain fixed on some remote object.

Personal distance

We carry a protective bubble defining our personal distance,
20   which allows us to stay protected and untouched by others. Personal distance ranges from 18 inches to about 4 feet. In the close phase, people can still hold or grasp each other, but only by extending their arms. We can then take into our protective bubble certain individuals – for example, loved
25   ones. In the far phase, you can touch another person only if you both extend your arms. This far phase is the extent to which you can physically get your hands on things; hence, it defines in one sense the limits of your physical control over others. At times, we may detect breath odor, but generally at
30   this distance etiquette demands that we direct our breath to some neutral corner so as not to offend.

Social distance

At the social distance, ranging from 4 to 12 feet, you lose the visual detail you had in the personal distance. The close phase is the distance at which you conduct impersonal business or interact at a social
35   gathering. The far phase is the distance at which you stand when someone says, "Stand away so I can look at you." At this distance,

The Structure of Academic Text

4 Defining language Ⓦ Ⓥ

A common way to define a term is to use the following sentence structure:
plural noun + *are* + plural noun + *that* + present tense verb

A Notice the way that *emblems* is defined in this reading:

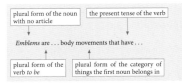

B Look at the definition of the other seven terms that you highlighted in Task 2. Which of them are defined in the same way as *emblems*?

C The four terms not defined in the same way as *emblems* can easily be defined that way. Rewrite them using the formula.

5 Signaling examples Ⓦ Ⓡ

Look at some different ways that writers introduce or "signal" that they are giving the reader examples.

for example	for instance	such as	an example of X is
including	X include(s)	examples include	

In a text that contains a large number of examples, you can expect the writer to vary his or her language and use several different ways to signal them. When you write a text with a lot of examples, vary your language too.

A Look back at the examples that you highlighted in Task 2. Find and circle any language that signals the examples. How many different types of signals did you find?

B Writers don't always start an example with a signal. Underline places in the text where examples follow the definition without a signal.

> **Extensive scaffolding** activities teach students the **structure of academic writing**.

C Complete the following sentences with the most appropriate verb from Part A. Use the correct verb form and tense.

1. The political situation in Western Africa is _____ rapidly. Soon there will be no law and order there.
2. Be careful how you wash that shirt. It may _____ .
3. After a while, the shaking from the earthquake began to _____ .
4. We are slowly _____ natural resources by consuming so much.
5. Over time, if you leave an area of carpet exposed to sunlight for too long, it will begin to _____ .

3 Paraphrasing Ⓦ Ⓡ

Sometimes you paraphrase so that you can use someone else's ideas in your essay writing (see Paraphrasing on page 80). However, when you read an important or difficult piece of text, it is also a good idea to try to paraphrase it to get a deeper understanding of it. By rewriting it, you prove to yourself that you have really understood it. This will also help you later if you have to recall the ideas from the text in a test.

A Study this paraphrase of Paragraph 2. Work with a partner and make a list of the changes.

In a study involving approximately 170,000 people from 16 countries, researcher Ronald Inglehart found that there was not much difference between the happiness and satisfaction felt by older and younger people. This may come as a surprise to many people, who believe that after about the age of 65, most elderly people must have miserable lives. They point out that these people have less money to spend, can't get work when they want to, suffer from poor heath, have poor memories, and have less energy than they used to have. Further, they assume that death is never very far from the elderly's thoughts because they have probably already seen some of their friends and family die.

B Reread page 80 to remind yourself of what steps to take when paraphrasing and how to paraphrase appropriately. Work with a partner and write a paraphrase of Paragraph 8.

C Work alone and write a paraphrase of Paragraph 6.

D Compare your paraphrase with a partner's. Notice the differences. Choose one of your paraphrases and work together to improve it.

> Students learn **key writing skills** such as paraphrasing and avoiding plagiarism. This early focus **prepares students** for later extended writing tasks.

Immersive Skill Building

Reading 1

EARLY ADULTHOOD

Just when adulthood begins is difficult to say. In a legal sense, adult status is often granted by governments – at age 18 for some activities or at age 21 for others. Psychologically speaking, adulthood is marked by two possibilities that at first seem contradictory: (1) independence, in the sense of taking responsibility for one's actions and no longer being tied to parents and (2) interdependence, in the sense of building new commitments and intimacies in interpersonal relationships.

In the past, there was little argument that adulthood abruptly followed the end of adolescence. However, some developmental psychologists have begun to argue recently that there is an in-between period when the individual is no longer an adolescent, but has also not yet taken on full adulthood status and independence. This period has been called **emerging adulthood**, a term coined in 2000 by developmental psychologist J. J. Arnett in a much cited article in *Psychology Today*. According to Arnett, young people from their late teens to their late twenties are increasingly going through an experimental period of self-exploration. They are delaying marriage and experimenting with work and love. They are also likely to still be somewhat dependent on their parents, who may continue to give them both some financial and emotional support.

emerging adulthood
a term used by some to describe a time when one is no longer an adolescent and not yet fully an adult

Chapter 4 Adulth

The full-color **design mirrors university textbooks**, ensuring that students not only practice reading authentic texts, but also receive an **authentic university experience.**

Throughout each unit, **explanatory boxes describe each skill** and help **students understand why it is important.**

3 Guessing meaning from context V R

Although there may be many words in a text that you do not know, you do not want to continually stop and look up words in the dictionary. It is often possible to get a general idea of the meaning of a word or phrase (and that is all you really need in order to continue reading) by looking at its full context. This means that your eyes need to travel back to the sentences that come before the word or phrase or forward to the sentence or sentences that follow it.

A Read the following passage from the text. Work with a partner and follow the instructions to answer the questions about the words in bold.

Many sorts of events can be stressors, including disasters, such as **hurricanes** or **tornadoes**; major life events, such as divorce or loss of a job; and **daily hassles**, such as having to wait in line at the supermarket when you need to be somewhere else in 10 minutes. What all these events have **in common** is that they interfere with our **accustomed** way of life.

1. If you know what a *disaster* is, you can guess what a *hurricane* or a *tornado* might be. What do you think they are?
2. Sentence 1 states that examples of "major life events" are divorce and losing a job. This is contrasted with waiting in line at a supermarket, which is called a *daily hassle*. What does *hassle* therefore probably mean?
3. In Sentence 1, we read about three different types of stressors – *disasters*, *major life events*, and *hassles*. Sentence 2 says that they all have something *in common*. What does *in common* probably mean?
4. In Sentence 2, we read that stressors "interfere with" our *accustomed* way of life. Does *accustomed* refer to something routine or something unusual?

B Read the following two passages from the text and use the same type of thinking to work out the meanings of the words and phrases in bold. Work alone and then compare your answers with a partner's.

Seyle proposed that both humans and other animals react to any stressor in three stages, **collectively** known as the *general adaptation syndrome*. The first stage, when the person or animal first becomes aware of the stressor, is the *alarm reaction*. In this stage the organism becomes highly **alert and aroused**, energized by a burst of **epinephrine**.

collectively _____

alert and aroused _____

epinephrine _____

Academic Vocabulary and Writing

> **4** The Academic Word List
>
> In academic writing and speech, certain words are used more frequently than in general writing and speech. Studies have shown that some of these words appear in academic language regardless of the academic subject matter. One researcher, Averil Coxhead of the University of Wellington, New Zealand, has created a list of these words, called the Academic Word List.
>
> **A** Match an Academic Word List word from the text with a word or phrase of similar meaning in the right column.
>
>   1. encountered (Line 3)   **a.** very important
>   2. thereby (Line 8)   **b.** made smaller
>   3. major (Line 14)   **c.** seemingly
>   4. induced (Line 16)   **d.** in this way
>   5. apparently (Line 41)   **e.** showed
>   6. minimized (Line 43)   **f.** fall
>   7. demonstrated (Line 47)   **g.** made to happen
>   8. duration (Line 52)   **h.** met
>   9. data (Line 67)   **i.** information
>   10. decline (Line 70)   **j.** length of time
>
> **B** Use eight of the words from the Academic Word List above to complete the following short text.
>
> Stress comes about when a _____ change takes place
> in a person's life. _____ from research suggest that when the
> _____ of the stress is long and the stress is _____
> continually, then the chance of developing an illness is high. Several experiments
> have _____ that the immune system reacts to stress. This reaction
> _____ causes a _____ in the immune system's
> effectiveness. However, there are also indications that the effects of stress can be
> _____ if people react to stress in an active way.
>
> **Chapter 1** *The Influence of Mind over Body*

Academic vocabulary development is **critical to student success**. Each unit includes **intensive vocabulary practice**, including words from the Academic Word List.

> **NOW WRITE**
>
> Structuring a comparison-contrast essay
>
> > There are two main ways that you can structure a comparison-contrast essay. In the first way, the block method, you write about several different topics relating to item A and then write about the same topics for item B. As you write about B, you make comparisons and contrasts between A and B. In the second method, the switching method, you write on each topic and keep switching from talking about A to talking about B in each section.
> >
> > | **Block Method** | **Switching Method** |
> > | --- | --- |
> > | Introduction | Introduction |
> > | Topic 1 about item A | Topic 1 about item A |
> > | Topic 2 about item A | Topic 1 about item B |
> > | Topic 3 about item A | Topic 2 about item A |
> > | Topic 1 about item B | Topic 2 about item B |
> > | Topic 2 about item B | Topic 3 about item A |
> > | Topic 3 about item B | Topic 3 about item B |
> > | Conclusion | Conclusion |
>
> **A** Review your freewriting, the chart you created on page 106, and your paraphrases. Sort through the different ideas you could write about. Then formulate your thesis. (See The Parts of an Essay on pages 26–27 for discussion of a thesis and thesis statements.)
>
> **B** Write an introductory paragraph that gives the reader some background information about the two periods that you have chosen to compare and contrast.
>
> **C** At the end of your introduction, write a thesis statement that prepares the reader for the body of your essay and the different ideas that you are going to include.
>
> **D** Decide which type of structure you are going to give your essay: Block Method or Switching Method. Then make a brief outline of the body of your essay.
>
> **E** Write the rest of your essay. Remember, a first draft does not have to be perfect. A first draft is just a beginning point. It provides you with some text that you can change until you are satisfied with the final product.
>
> **Chapter 4** *Adulthood* **107**

Students complete each unit by **applying their skills** and knowledge in an extended writing task that **replicates university coursework.**

To the student

Welcome to *Academic Encounters 4 Reading and Writing: Human Behavior*!

The *Academic Encounters* series gets its name because in this series you will encounter, or meet, the kinds of *academic* texts (lectures and readings), *academic* language (grammar and vocabulary), and *academic* tasks (taking tests, writing papers, and giving presentations) that you will encounter when you study an academic subject area in English. The goal of the series, therefore, is to prepare you for that encounter.

The approach of *Academic Encounters 4 Reading and Writing: Human Behavior* may be different from what you are used to in your English studies. In this book, you are asked to study an academic subject area and be responsible for learning that information, in the same way as you might study in a college or university course. You will find that as you study this information, you will at the same time improve your English language proficiency and develop the skills that you will need to be successful when you come to study in your own academic subject area in English.

In *Academic Encounters 4 Reading and Writing: Human Behavior*, for example, you will learn:

- how to read academic texts
- ways to think critically about what you read
- how to write in an academic style
- methods of preparing for tests
- strategies for dealing with new vocabulary
- note-taking and study techniques

This course is designed to help you study in English in *any* subject matter. However, because during the study of this book, you will learn a lot of new information about research findings and theories related to human behavior, you may feel that by the end you have enough background information to one day take and be successful in an introductory course in psychology or communications in English.

We certainly hope that you find *Academic Encounters 4 Reading and Writing: Human Behavior* useful. We also hope that you will find it to be enjoyable. It is important to remember that the most successful learning takes place when you enjoy what you are studying and find it interesting.

Author's acknowledgments

For the last ten years, in my work as an editor, I have been guiding other authors in writing new editions of their works. This time, as they say, the shoe was on the other foot. Going through the process of writing a second edition of my own has made me realize how challenging it is to look at something that one has written and that is now in print and seemingly immutable, and to imagine how it could and should be different. Fortunately, the writer is not alone in this endeavor—looking at the same text with much greater objectivity is one's editor. So my first thanks go to Mary Ann Maynard, my development editor, who not only helped me write more elegantly and economically, but who also helped me through the winnowing process of deciding what stays and what goes, and what is to be added.

Much credit should also go to Christopher Sol Cruz for taking on the daunting challenge of helping to envision the second edition of the *Academic Encounters* series and for managing the editorial process. Helping him were Brandon Carda and Robin Berenbaum, to whom thanks are also due for their hard work.

At Cambridge, many different people also contributed to the creation of the second edition. Thanks go to Sheryl Olinsky Borg, Publishing Manager; Caitlin Mara, Associate Managing Editor; Quin Paseka, Editorial Assistant; Heather McCarron, Production Operations Supervisor; Holly Haydash, Project Controller; and John Brezinsky, Senior Product Manager.

Finally, I want to acknowledge the help of my family. When I wrote the first edition of this book, my two sons, Daniel and Elliott, were both under ten years old, and I wrote in the acknowledgments to that book that they were "a delightful distraction." More than ten years later, they provided "delightful assistance." They were able to help with many aspects of the writing: critiquing readings and tasks, doing some research, formatting texts, and preparing answer keys. My wife, Chris, too pitched in to make it a true family affair. The summer of 2011 was much more bearable because of it. Thanks Daniel, Elliott, and Chris.

Bernard Seal

Publisher's acknowledgments

The first edition of *Academic Encounters* has been used by many teachers in many institutions all around the world. Over the years, countless instructors have passed on feedback about the series, all of which has proven invaluable in helping to direct the vision for the second edition. More formally, a number of reviewers also provided us with a detailed analysis of the series, and we are especially grateful for their insights. We would therefore like to extend particular thanks to the following instructors:

Matthew Gordon Ray Courtney, The University of Auckland, New Zealand

Nancy Hamadou, Pima Community College – West Campus, Tucson, AZ

Yoneko Kanaoka, Hawaii English Language Program at the University of Hawaii at Manoa; Honolulu, Hawaii

Margaret V. Layton, University of Nevada, Reno, Nevada

Dot MacKenzie, Kuwait University, Sabah Al-Salem University City, Kuwait

Jennifer Wharton, Leeward Community College, Pearl City, Hawaii

Unit 1
Mind, Body, and Health

In this unit you will look at the relationship between human behavior and health. In Chapter 1, you will learn that mental and emotional states, especially feelings of stress, may influence your physical health. In Chapter 2, you will see that illness can sometimes be prevented or controlled if people change their behavior. You will look at research that shows that people live longer and healthier lives if they relax, don't smoke, exercise, and have a spiritual dimension to their lives.

Contents

In Unit 1, you will read and write about the following topics.

Skills

In Unit 1, you will practice the following skills.

R Reading Skills	**W** Writing Skills
Thinking about the topic Predicting Reading for main ideas Thinking about what you already know Scanning Thinking critically Personalizing the topic Skimming Increasing reading speed Comprehension after speed reading	Parallel sentence structure Hedging Comparing Understanding paragraph structure
V Vocabulary Skills	**A** Academic Success Skills
Guessing meaning from context Dealing with unknown words The Academic Word List Describing change Scientific terms Describing experimental results	Highlighting Preparing for a test Answering multiple-choice questions Taking notes using arrows Answering true/false questions Preparing for a short-answer test Writing short answers to test questions

Learning Outcomes

Write an essay on health risk factors.

Previewing the Unit

Before reading a unit (or chapter) of a textbook, it is a good idea to preview the contents page and think about the topics that will be covered. This will give you an overview of how the unit is organized and what it is going to be about.

Read the contents page of Unit 1 on page 2 and do the following activities.

Chapter 1: The Influence of Mind over Body

A The focus of Chapter 1 is stress. Work with a partner and make lists for the following three categories. Be prepared to explain your choices to the class.

- five stressful jobs
- five unstressful jobs
- five illnesses frequently caused by stress

B Work with a partner and discuss whether you think the following would be good or bad advice. Put a check (✓) next to the advice that you think is good.

____ **1.** If you know you are going to be in a stressful situation, the best thing to do is to relax and do nothing until it actually happens.

____ **2.** If you get a serious illness, adopt a fighting spirit. Believe you will overcome it.

____ **3.** Avoid having any stress in your life at any time.

____ **4.** Try not to get depressed because depression can affect your physical health.

Chapter 2: Lifestyle and Health

A In Chapter 2, you will learn about behaviors that can be harmful to your health, such as smoking, and healthful behaviors, such as exercise. Work with a partner and interview each other for a few minutes on the topics of smoking and exercise. Ask questions such as these:

1. Is smoking common in your country? Do you smoke? If yes, how many cigarettes a day? When did you start? If not, have you ever smoked and managed to quit? How did you quit?

2. What forms of exercise are popular in your country? Do many people walk, bike, run, or exercise in gyms? What do you do for exercise?

B Change partners and interview each other about what you do to keep fit and healthy.

Chapter 1
The Influence of Mind over Body

Thinking about the topic ®

> Thinking about a topic before you read helps provide a context for the reading and
> can make it easier to understand.

According to a famous study by American psychologists Holmes and Rahe over 40 years
ago, different life events cause different levels of stress. Holmes and Rahe worked out a
scale in which the most stressful event – the death of a husband or wife – was given
a value of 100 points. Less stressful events were given values ranging from 99 points to
1 point.

A Look at the stressful events listed. In the left-hand column, rank the events from most
stressful (*1*) to least stressful (*8*). Compare your answers with a partner's and explain
why you rated one event more stressful than another.

Rank	Event	Value
	Getting married	
	Moving into a new residence	
	Death of a close friend	
	Going on vacation	
	Being fired from work	
	Getting divorced	
	Getting a parking ticket	
	Gaining a new family member (e.g., through birth or adoption)	

B Now, with your partner, agree on a value for each stressful event, using the Holmes
and Rahe 100-point scale. Write this value in the column on the right.

C Turn to page 10, where you will find the values that Holmes and Rahe gave to different
events (Figure 1.1). Compare your values with theirs and discuss what surprises you in
their list.

D Discuss the ways in which you think the results might be different if the research were
done today.

E Discuss the ways in which you think the results might be different if the research were
done in your country.

Reading 1

WHAT IS STRESS?

The term **stress** has been defined in several different ways. Sometimes the term is applied to stimuli or events in our environment that make physical and emotional demands on us, and sometimes it is applied to our emotional and physical reactions to such stimuli. In this
5 discussion, we will refer to the environmental stimuli or events as **stressors** and to the emotional and physical reactions as stress.

Many sorts of events can be stressors, including disasters, such as hurricanes or tornadoes; major life events, such as divorce or the loss of a job; and daily hassles, such as having to wait in line at the
10 supermarket when you need to be somewhere else in 10 minutes. What all these events have in common is that they interfere with or threaten our accustomed way of life. When we encounter such stressors, we must pull together our mental and physical resources in order to deal with the challenge. How well we succeed in doing so will
15 determine how serious a toll the stress will take on our mental and physical well-being.

Reacting to stressors

The Canadian physiologist Hans Seyle has been the most influential writer on stress. Seyle proposed that both humans and other animals react to any stressor in three stages, collectively known as the *general*
20 *adaptation syndrome*. The first stage, when the person or animal first becomes aware of the stressor, is the *alarm reaction*. In this stage the organism becomes highly alert and aroused, energized by a burst of epinephrine. After the alarm reaction comes the stage of *resistance*, as the organism tries to adapt to the stressful stimulus or to escape
25 from it. If these efforts are successful, the state of the organism returns to normal. If the organism cannot adapt to the continuing stress, however, it enters a stage of *exhaustion*, or collapse.

stress an emotional or physical reaction to demanding events or stimuli

stressors events or stimuli that cause stress

Seyle developed his model of the general adaptation syndrome as a result of research with rats and other animals. In rats, certain stressors, such as painful tail-pulling, consistently led to the same sorts of stress reactions. In humans, however, it is harder to predict what will be stressful to a particular person at a particular time. Whether a particular stimulus will be stressful depends on the person's subjective appraisal of that stimulus. How threatening is it? How well have I handled this sort of thing in the past? How well will I be able to handle it this time? For one person, being called on to give a talk in front of a class is a highly stressful stimulus that will immediately produce such elements as a pounding heart and a dry mouth. For another person, being called on to give a talk is not threatening at all, but facing a deadline to complete a term paper is extremely stressful. In humans, moreover, the specific stress reaction is likely to vary widely; some stressful situations give rise predominantly to emotions of fear, some give rise to anger, and some give rise to helplessness and depression.

For some, not winning may be a stressful event; for others, coming second may not be a stressor at all.

1 Highlighting Ⓐ Ⓥ Ⓡ

Highlighting makes important information stand out so that you can find it easily when you go back to the text to study for a test. Systematically using different colored highlighter pens can make the review process easier. For example, you can use one color for key terms and another for their definitions. You can use one color for a main idea and another for supporting details.

A Find the following words and phrases where they appear in either italics or boldface and highlight them.

stress	alarm reaction
stressors	resistance
general adaptation syndrome	exhaustion

B Use a different-colored highlighter and highlight the following:

- a definition of *stress* and *stressors*
- a statement about what all stressors have in common
- a description of Stage 1 of the general adaptation syndrome
- a description of Stage 2 of the general adaptation syndrome
- a description of Stage 3 of the general adaptation syndrome
- the sentence containing the main idea of the last paragraph

C Compare your answers with a partner's.

2 Preparing for a test Ⓐ Ⓡ

When you prepare for a test, you need to pay close attention to understanding key terms and main ideas. If you have highlighted these in the text, pay careful attention to those parts as you review it. They are the parts of the text that you are most likely to be tested on.

Look back at the text that you highlighted in "What Is Stress?" Work with a partner and use the information you highlighted to say how you would answer these four questions that might be on a test about this text.

1. What is a *stressor*?
2. What are the three different stages of the general adaptation syndrome?
3. Why are going on vacation and getting divorced both stressful to some degree?
4. What is one major difference in the way that rats react to a stressful event and the way that humans do?

3 Guessing meaning from context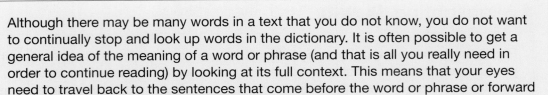

Although there may be many words in a text that you do not know, you do not want to continually stop and look up words in the dictionary. It is often possible to get a general idea of the meaning of a word or phrase (and that is all you really need in order to continue reading) by looking at its full context. This means that your eyes need to travel back to the sentences that come before the word or phrase or forward to the sentence or sentences that follow it.

A Read the following passage from the text. Work with a partner and follow the instructions to answer the questions about the words in bold.

Many sorts of events can be stressors, including disasters, such as **hurricanes** or **tornadoes**; major life events, such as divorce or loss of a job; and **daily hassles**, such as having to wait in line at the supermarket when you need to be somewhere else in 10 minutes. What all these events have **in common** is that they interfere with our **accustomed** way of life.

1. If you know what a *disaster* is, you can guess what a *hurricane* or a *tornado* might be. What do you think they are?
2. Sentence 1 states that examples of "major life events" are divorce and losing a job. This is contrasted with waiting in line at a supermarket, which is called a *daily hassle*. What does *hassle* therefore probably mean?
3. In Sentence 1, we read about three different types of stressors – *disasters*, *major life events*, and *hassles*. Sentence 2 says that they all have something *in common*. What does *in common* probably mean?
4. In Sentence 2, we read that stressors "interfere with" our *accustomed* way of life. Does *accustomed* refer to something routine or something unusual?

B Read the following two passages from the text and use the same type of thinking to work out the meanings of the words and phrases in bold. Work alone and then compare your answers with a partner's.

Seyle proposed that both humans and other animals react to any stressor in three stages, **collectively** known as the *general adaptation syndrome*. The first stage, when the person or animal first becomes aware of the stressor, is the *alarm reaction*. In this stage the organism becomes highly **alert and aroused**, energized by a burst of **epinephrine**.

collectively _____

alert and aroused _____

epinephrine _____

Whether a particular stimulus will be stressful depends on the person's **subjective appraisal** of that stimulus. How **threatening** is it? How well have I **handled** this sort of thing in the past? How well will I be able to handle it this time? For one person, **being called on** to give a talk in front of a class is a highly stressful stimulus that will immediately produce such elements as a **pounding** heart and a dry mouth.

subjective appraisal _____

threatening _____

handled _____

being called on _____

pounding _____

4 Parallel sentence structure Ⓦ Ⓡ

Good writers often use parallel sentence structure. This means that they use the same pattern of words either within the same sentence or in a following sentence or sentences. This can help readers follow what a writer wants to say.

A Find parallel sentence structures in the text.

  1. Find the second part of a parallel structure in Paragraph 1 that contrasts different ways of defining the term *stress*. The first part begins: "Sometimes the term is applied to . . ."

  _____

  2. Find two examples of parallel sentence structure in Paragraph 4 beginning with the phrases below.

  a. For one person, . . .

  _____

  b. . . . some stressful situations give rise to . . .

  _____

B Practice using parallel sentence structure to give your own examples of different kinds of stressors. Write two sentences. The beginning of each sentence is provided for you.

Some stressors _____

_____

Other stressors _____

_____

Fig. 1.1 The Holmes and Rahe social readjustment rating scale

Life Event	Mean Value
Death of a spouse	100
Divorce	73
Death of a close family member	63
Major personal injury or illness	53
Marriage	50
Being fired from work	47
Retiring from work	45
Major change in health of a family member	44
Pregnancy	40
Gaining a new family member *(e.g., through birth, adoption, etc.)*	39
Major change in financial state *(e.g., having a lot more or less money)*	38
Death of a close friend	37
Taking out a mortgage or loan for a major purchase *(e.g., a home or business)*	31
Major change in responsibilities at work *(e.g., promotion, demotion)*	29
Son or daughter leaving home *(e.g., marriage, attending college)*	29
Beginning or ceasing formal schooling	26
Major changes in living conditions *(e.g., building a home, remodeling a home)*	25
Trouble with the boss	23
Major change in working hours or conditions	20
Change in residence	20
Changing to a new school	20
Taking out a small loan *(e.g., for a car, TV, freezer, etc.)*	17
Vacation	13
Christmas	12
Minor violations of the law *(e.g., traffic tickets, jaywalking)*	11

Source: Adapted from Holmes and Rahe

Predicting ®

Trying to predict what information will be in a text before you read is a good habit. It motivates you to read the text carefully to find out if your predictions were correct.

A Preview the subheadings in this text. With a partner, discuss how these subheadings might relate to an individual's ability to cope with stress.

B Read the following situations (described in the text) and predict how the questions that accompany them will be answered. Compare your answers with a partner's and discuss again what you predict will be said in the text under each subheading.

1. Imagine two young lawyers are told on a Friday that they have only the weekend to prepare a report on a complex case. One feels anxiety; the other feels it is a challenge and an opportunity to prove her worth. Which lawyer has a personality that is better suited to cope well with stress?
   a. the anxious lawyer
   b. the lawyer who feels it is an opportunity

2. Two rats are given exactly the same amount of electric shock. One rat is able to turn off the shock; the other one can only be passive and must wait for the shock to stop. Which rat do you think has a worse physical reaction to the shock?
   a. the rat that has more control over the situation
   b. the rat that is passive and has less control

3. Two rats are given exactly the same amount of electric shock. However, one rat hears a buzzer 10 seconds before each shock, while the other rat hears nothing. Which rat do you think has a worse physical reaction to the electric shock?
   a. the rat that hears the buzzer and knows that the shock is coming
   b. the rat that gets no warning and cannot predict when the shock is going to come

4. Which stressful situation do you think is easier to cope with?
   a.the sudden death of a loved one
   b. the expected death of a loved one after a long illness

5. A professor sometimes gives scheduled quizzes and sometimes gives surprise quizzes. Which do you think is more stressful for students?
   a. scheduled quizzes
   b. surprise quizzes

C Compare your predictions with a partner's and discuss again what you think might be said in the text under each subheading.

Reading 2

COPING WITH STRESS

It is Friday evening and two young lawyers get phone calls at home. The trial date for an important case has been moved up. Both of the lawyers will now have to prepare a report for the case by Monday morning. It is a threatening situation for both. Each must do extensive
5 research and write a complex document of some 40 pages, all in a single weekend. Furthermore, each knows that her work will be evaluated by the firm's partners, and how well she does may greatly influence her future in the firm.

One of the lawyers finds the situation extremely stressful; she feels
10 tremendous anxiety, experiences headaches and stomach upset, and has difficulty working. She somehow manages to produce a report, but she is not at all happy with it. The other lawyer, although she too feels the pressure of the situation, sees it not so much as a threat but as a challenge – an opportunity to show how good she is. She moves
15 into the firm's offices for the weekend and, sleeping only three hours a night, completes a brilliant report with a clear mind and a surge of energy. As this example helps illustrate, stress is caused not so much by events themselves as by the ways in which people perceive and react to events.

Degree of control

20 An important influence on people's ability to cope with stressful situations is the degree of control that they feel they can exercise over the situation. Both animals and humans have been found to cope better with painful or threatening stimuli when they feel they can exercise some degree of control rather than being passive and helpless
25 victims. Such a sense of control can help minimize the negative consequences of stress, both psychological and physical. In one well-known experiment, Jay Weiss administered electric shocks to pairs of rats. In each pair, one of the two animals was given a degree of control over the situation; it could reach through a hole in the cage and press
30 a panel that would turn off the shock both for itself and for its partner. Thus, the two rats received exactly the same number of shocks, but one was passive and helpless, and the other was in control. After a continuous 21-hour session, the animals were sacrificed and their stomachs examined for ulcers. Those rats that could exert control had
35 much less ulceration than their helpless partners.

The ability to control painful stimuli often benefits humans, too. For example, the loud music coming into your ears from your iPod is probably not stressful; in fact, it's quite enjoyable. But the same music coming from your neighbor's house can be terribly irritating and 40 stressful. Merely knowing that one can control a noise makes it less bothersome. That's one reason why your loud music does not bother you – you know you can turn it off.

Predictability

Even when you cannot control them, unpleasant events tend to be less stressful if they are predictable – if you at least know when they will 45 occur. This was demonstrated by Weiss in another study with rats. One group of rats heard a buzzer about 10 seconds before they would receive a shock; although the animals could not escape the shock, at least they had a chance to prepare themselves for the expected pain. A second group of rats received no such warnings; the shocks came 50 unpredictably. Weiss found that the rats that were forewarned of the shocks developed fewer ulcers than the rats that were not forewarned. This finding has parallels in human life. The death of a loved one, for example, is usually less traumatic when it is anticipated than when it is unexpected. On a less tragic level, many students find surprise quizzes 55 to be more upsetting than scheduled quizzes that they can prepare for.

Experiment showing one rat being warned by a buzzer that a shock is coming, while the other rat hears nothing.

Fig. 1.2 Health consequences of a loss of control

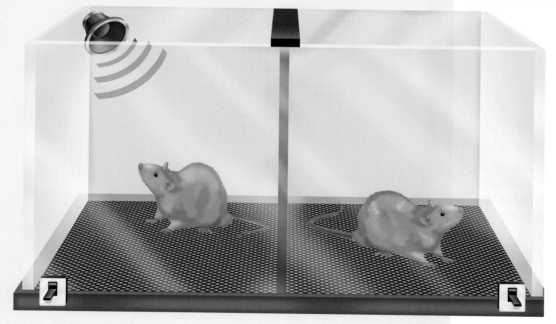

Source: **Adapted from Weiss**

Personality factors

Are some people generally better than others at coping with stress? Research suggests that the answer is yes – that there is a certain kind of person who has a relatively **stress-resistant personality**. The leading researcher in this field has been Suzanne Kobasa.
60 Dr. Kobasa found that people who cope well with stress tend to have three characteristics: They are committed to what they are doing, they feel in control (rather than powerless), and they welcome moderate amounts of change and challenge. In studies of people facing stressful situations, Kobasa and her associates found that those with stress-
65 resistant personalities – that is, those who are high in commitment, control, and challenge – experience fewer physical illnesses than those whose personalities are less hardy.

stress-resistant personality
characteristics that enable a person to cope well in stressful situations

Some people have personalities that make them unaffected by stressors.

Until quite recently, it was generally believed that to maintain good health people should strive to avoid stressors in their lives. Such
70 a strategy can be quite limiting, however. The desire to avoid stress may also lead people to avoid potentially beneficial changes in their lives, such as job changes or promotions. Moreover, the attempt to avoid stress is often unrealistic. How, for example, can a person avoid such shocks as a parent's death? In fact, if people do not confront a
75 certain amount of stress in their lives, they will end up being bored and unstimulated, which also can be physically harmful. In the last analysis, each person needs to come to terms with stress in his or her own way, sometimes trying to avoid it, but sometimes accepting it or even seeking it out as a challenge to be mastered.

1 Reading for main ideas ®

A reading often has one central question that it is trying to answer. The answers to this question are the main ideas in the text. Identifying the main ideas and the specific details that support them is probably your primary task in reading a text.

A Look at the title of this reading: "Coping with Stress." Skim through the reading. What is the central question that this text is trying to answer?

  a. Why do people feel stress?

  b. What happens to people who feel stress?

  c. What are some ways to reduce stress?

B Look at the three subheadings in this text. Match the subheadings to each of the following main ideas.

  a. It is easier to cope with stress if you are able to do something to try to stop the cause of the stress.

  b. It is easier to cope with stress if you are a person who welcomes challenge.

  c. It is easier to cope with stress if you have some advance notice that a stressful event is going to happen.

C Five situations described in the text and introduced in the "Preparing to Read" activity on page 10 support one of the main ideas, a, b, or c, in B above. Match each situation to the main idea it supports. Write *a*, *b*, or *c*, on the line next to the situation.

  ____ **1.** the anxious lawyer and the lawyer who sees a challenge in writing the report

  ____ **2.** the active rat and the passive rat

  ____ **3.** the rat that hears the buzzer and the rat that hears nothing

  ____ **4.** the sudden death of a loved one and the expected death of a loved one

  ____ **5.** scheduled quizzes and surprise quizzes

D Use the answers in Steps A–C above to write a short paragraph restating the information in this reading. Use the paragraph structure below to write the paragraph on a separate piece of paper.

  According to research, there appear to be three main ways to _____ . First, _____ . For example, experiments with rats _____ . Second, _____ . Thus, students prefer _____ . Finally, _____ .

2 Dealing with unknown words Ⓥ

You are often going to come across unknown words when you read a college text. There are several strategies that you can use when this happens:

1. Ignore the word. You can understand enough of the text without knowing this word.
2. Quickly guess the approximate meaning of this word from its context.
3. Look at the parts of the word and see if you can work out its approximate meaning from its parts.
4. Look the word up in a dictionary when you feel that knowing it is necessary to understand the main ideas of the text.

A Find the following words and phrases in the text. With a partner, decide which strategy you should use to determine the meaning of the boldfaced word, and why. Write the number of the strategy (*1–4*) on the line.

____ **a.** with . . . a **surge** of energy. (Line 16)

____ **b.** In one . . . experiment, [he] **administered** electric shocks . . . (Line 27)

____ **c.** . . . the animals were **sacrificed** and their stomachs examined . . . (Line 33)

____ **d.** Those rats that could **exert** control . . . (Line 34)

____ **e.** . . . music . . . can be terribly **irritating** . . . (Line 39)

____ **f.** . . . knowing that one can control a noise . . . it less **bothersome**. (Line 41)

____ **g.** . . . the rats that were **forewarned** . . . (Line 51)

____ **h.** . . . less **traumatic** when it is anticipated . . . (Line 53)

____ **i.** . . . whose personalities are **hardy**. (Line 67)

____ **j.** . . . people should **strive** to avoid stressors . . . (Line 69)

B In the cases that you chose to use strategies 2 or 3, what did you guess the approximate meaning of the word to be?

3 Answering multiple-choice questions Ⓐ Ⓡ

> Answering multiple-choice questions can be tricky. It is very important to read the questions carefully. Look to see if the answer is something that is true or *not* true. Look for words like *always*, *never*, and *all* in an answer. Often when these words appear, the answer they are in is not the right one. And if you have no idea of the correct answer, often the longest answer is the correct one.

Answer these multiple-choice questions about the reading.

1. Which of the following is not true for the two lawyers who had to write reports over the weekend?
   a. Both lawyers were nervous.
   b. Both lawyers produced excellent reports.
   c. One lawyer felt sick while writing the report.
   d. Both lawyers finished their reports by the given deadline.

2. Which of the following is true of all the rats in both of Weiss's experiments?
   a. They received the same amount of electric shock.
   b. They heard a buzzer before they were shocked.
   c. They had some degree of control over when they were shocked.
   d. They had the same degree of ulcerations following the experiments.

3. Which of the following statements is not true for people who have a "stress-resistant personality"?
   a. They have feelings of powerlessness.
   b. They welcome a challenge.
   c. They are hardy.
   d. They commit themselves to what they are doing.

4. Which statement is true according to the reading?
   a. It is possible to avoid all stressors in one's life.
   b. Benefits always come to people who take on stressful challenges.
   c. In the past, people generally believed one should try to avoid stress.
   d. A certain amount of stress is never good for you.

1 Thinking about what you already know

> The more you know about a topic, the easier it is to read information on that topic. Asking yourself questions about the topic of the text before you start reading will help you recall what you already know.

How much do you know about the way the human body works? Discuss these questions with a partner or the class.

1. Which parts of the body are most often associated with the following illnesses: *arthritis, asthma, migraine, headaches, ulcers*?
2. What is cancer? What parts of the body are often attacked by cancer?
3. What is the difference between viruses and bacteria?
4. What is the immune system? How does it function? What happens when the immune system is not functioning properly?
5. What do you think *psychoimmunology* might mean?
6. What relationship do you think scientists might find between stress and one's susceptibility to disease?

2 Scanning ®

> Scanning involves looking quickly through a text to find a specific word or piece of information. There are often times when it is necessary to do this, such as when studying for a test or writing a paper, so it is a useful skill to practice.

This text and the boxed "Post-Traumatic Stress Disorder (PTSD)" address the relationship between being under stress and becoming ill. Scan the text quickly to find the following.

1. Illnesses that can be caused by stress (Par. 1)
2. Jobs that are highly stressful (Par. 2)
3. The field of research that studies the influence of psychological factors on the immune system (Par. 4)
4. The researcher who studied the effect of depression in men on cancer rates (Par. 6)
5. Two other names for Post-Traumatic Stress Disorder (PTSD) before it was named PTSD (boxed text on page 20)

Reading 3

STRESS AND ILLNESS

In many stressful situations, the body's response can improve our performance – we become more energetic, more alert, and better able to take effective action. But when stress is encountered continually, the body's reactions are more likely to be harmful than helpful to
5 us. As will be seen later in this unit, the production of stress-related hormones seems to make people more susceptible to heart disease. And stress reactions can reduce the disease-fighting effectiveness of the body's immune system, thereby increasing susceptibility to illnesses, ranging from colds to cancer. Other diseases that can
10 result at least in part from stress include arthritis, asthma, migraine headaches, and ulcers. Workers who experience the greatest amount of job pressure have been found to be especially likely to suffer from a large number of illnesses. Moreover, many studies have shown that people who have experienced major changes in their lives are at an
15 unusually high risk for a variety of illnesses.

As an example of stress-induced illness, take the case of stomach ulcers, small lesions in the stomach wall that afflict one out of every twenty people at some point in their lives. Ulcers are a common
20 disorder among people who work in occupations that make heavy psychological demands, from assembly-line workers to air-traffic controllers. In such cases, stress tends to be the culprit. Stress leads to increased secretion of hydrochloric acid in the stomach.
25 Hydrochloric acid normally helps to break down foods during digestion, but in excess amounts it can eat away at the stomach lining, producing ulcers.

People with very stressful jobs may be more susceptible to illness.

Stress and cancer

One of the least understood diseases, and partly for that reason one of the most feared, is cancer, which is the second leading cause of
30 death in America. Medical scientists and researchers are still trying to understand the biological mechanisms of cell behavior that underlie the onset and development of cancer. However, studies seem to suggest that there may be links between emotions and cancer.

These links involve the functioning of the body's immune system,
35 a collection of billions of cells that travel through the bloodstream and defend the body against invasion by foreign agents, including bacteria and viruses, and against cells that become cancerous. Psychological factors can influence immune functioning and the field of research on these influences is called **psychoimmunology**. It
40 is believed that small cancers form frequently in everyone, but our

psychoimmunology
a field of study that investigates the effect of psychological factors on the immune system

immune system usually rejects them. However, prolonged stress may lead to elevated levels of corticosteroids and to lower levels of the neurotransmitter norepinephrine in the brain. These and other changes apparently make it harder for the immune system to reject cancer cells. When the organism copes with the stress in an active way, these changes in the immune system seem to be minimized; when the organism reacts with helplessness and depression, the changes are maximized.

POST-TRAUMATIC STRESS DISORDER (PTSD)

Post-traumatic stress disorder (PTSD) has a long history, although it was only in 1980 that it was defined as a specific illness with a specific diagnosis. For thousands of years, many soldiers came back from the battlefield complaining of a variety of symptoms. Some felt their heart beat faster and irregularly. Some shook uncontrollably. Some were easily startled by noise. And many kept having "flashbacks," imagining they were back on the battlefield facing the same horrors again and again. In World War I, it was called "shell shock." In World War II, it was called "battle fatigue." But it was not until after the Vietnam War that it was officially recognized as a definable disorder and called PTSD.

Today, it is also recognized that anyone, not just soldiers, may suffer from PTSD after experiencing or witnessing a horrific and violent event, such as the death and destruction following an earthquake, a train crash, or a bomb blast.

The existence of PTSD clearly suggests that the mind and the body are connected, as we see individuals suffering physical symptoms following emotional trauma. However, it is only very recently that researchers have uncovered a remarkable physical change in PTSD sufferers. In a breakthrough piece of research, published in May 2010, researchers at the University of Michigan say that they have discovered a genetic change that takes place in PTSD sufferers. This change, they claim, weakens PTSD sufferers' immune system and makes them more susceptible to a number of serious illnesses.

Animal studies

These links between stress, helplessness, immune function, and cancer
have been demonstrated experimentally in studies with animals.
In one study, conducted by Sklar and Anisman, three groups of
mice were injected with the same number of cancer cells. One
group was exposed to an electric shock that they could learn
to escape by jumping over a barrier to safety. A second group
was exposed to the same duration of shock, but had no
means of actively coping with the stress. The third group
was never shocked. The cancer grew the fastest and led
to the earliest death in the animals that had no means
of coping with their stress. In contrast, the animals that
could mount an effective escape did not differ in tumor
growth from those that had not been shocked at all.

Human studies

The link between stress, helplessness, and cancer has been
demonstrated in humans as well. In one dramatic study in
1981, Richard Shekelle and his co-workers studied over 2,000
men who had taken a psychological test that diagnoses depression
and other emotional states. Seventeen years later, the researcher
found that those men who had been highly depressed at the time
of the testing had twice the chance of dying of cancer as men who
had not been depressed. Since depressed people tend to drink more
alcohol or smoke more cigarettes, which in turn increases their risk
of cancer, Shekelle took this into account when he analyzed his data;
the association between depression and cancer still held, regardless of
drinking or smoking rates. In another study, widowed husbands were
found to have a decline in the function of their white blood cells – part
of the immune system – within two months of their wives' deaths.

There is also some evidence that people's emotions are involved
in cancer once it has begun. In a study of women who underwent
mastectomy for early-stage breast cancer, Greer found that women who
reacted to their diagnosis with either a fighting spirit or strong denial
were more likely to be free of disease eight years later than were women
who reacted with stoic acceptance or with feelings of helplessness.

Recommendations for treatment

Findings on the links between emotional reactions to stress and the
progression of cancer have given rise to some recommendations for
the treatment of cancer patients. In particular, programs that can help
give cancer patients a greater feeling of control over their destinies and
that can help them adopt a "fighting spirit" might just increase their
odds of survival. Although there is no solid evidence as yet that such
programs can in fact extend people's lives, developing such programs
remains an exciting frontier in health psychology.

The death of a loved one may be lead to depression, which is thought to increase one's risk of cancer.

1 Taking notes using arrows Ⓐ Ⓡ

Taking notes can help you capture the meaning of a long text in a small space. This makes it easier for you to review the text for a test. One way to make notes is to use arrows, which can be used in two main ways:

shows one thing causes or leads to another →

→ shows one thing results from another

↑ shows something increases   ↑↑ shows something increases a lot

↓ shows something decreases   ↓↓ shows something decreases a lot

A Use arrows to make notes from the following excerpts from the reading. The first one is done for you as an example.

1. In many stressful situations, the body's response can improve our performance – we become more energetic, more alert, and better able to take effective action.

   Many stressful situations → improved performance → ↑energy ↑alertness ↑ability to act

2. And stress reactions can reduce the disease-fighting effectiveness of the body's immune system, thereby increasing susceptibility to illnesses . . .

3. Ulcers are a common disorder among people who work in occupations that make heavy psychological demands. . . .

4. Stress leads to increased secretion of hydrochloric acid in the stomach. . . . in excess amounts it can eat away at the stomach lining, producing ulcers.

5. . . . prolonged stress may lead to elevated levels of corticosteroids and to lower levels of the neurotransmitter norepinephrine in the brain. These and other changes apparently make it harder for the immune system to reject cancer cells.

6. . . . depressed people tend to drink more alcohol or smoke more cigarettes, which in turn increases their risk of cancer . . .

7. . . . widowed husbands were found to have a decline in the function of their white blood cells . . .

B Compare your answers with a partner's.

2 Hedging Ⓦ Ⓡ

In much of academic writing, authors try to show connections between one event or state and another. However, it is often very difficult to prove that such a link, or connection, really exists or is always true. To show that the relationship is possible, not definite, writers use many different techniques, known collectively as "hedging language." Common examples include:

Modals *may, might, can, could*

Phrases *it is (un)likely that, it is possible that, there is some evidence that*

Verbs *seem to, tend to, appear to*

Adverbs *usually, in many cases, frequently, generally, possibly*

Quantifiers *some, most, a few*

A Circle the hedging language in the following excerpts from the reading.

1. In many stressful situations, the body's response can improve our performance . . .

2. . . . the production of stress-related hormones seems to make people more susceptible to heart disease.

3. Other diseases that can result at least in part from stress include . . .

4. However, studies seem to suggest that there may be links between emotions and cancer.

5. Since depressed people tend to drink more alcohol or smoke more cigarettes, which in turn increases their risk of cancer . . .

6. There is also some evidence that people's emotions are involved in cancer once it has begun.

7. . . . programs that can help give cancer patients a greater feeling of control over their destinies and that can help them adopt a "fighting spirit" might just increase their odds of survival.

B Compare your answers with a partner's.

3 Thinking critically ®

It is important to use your critical thinking skills when you read. This means that as you read you should continually be asking yourself what the writer is really saying. In particular, pay attention to words and phrases like *seems to*, *may be*, *it is likely that*, *can*, and *it is possible that*.

A The reading "Stress and Illness" and the boxed text "Post-Traumatic Stress Disorder" explore possible causal links between stress and illness and stress and cancer. Read the statements below. Put a check (✓) next to those statements which are true according to these readings.

___ **1.** Stressful situations sometimes have a positive effect.

___ **2.** People who experience a great deal of stress will develop a serious illness.

___ **3.** When air-traffic controllers get ulcers, the ulcers are caused by stress.

___ **4.** It is possible that there is a link between our emotional states and cancer.

___ **5.** Depression seems to increase your risk of getting cancer.

___ **6.** Smoking cigarettes and drinking alcohol causes cancer.

___ **7.** Reacting to news that you have cancer by adopting a stoic acceptance may lead to earlier death than if you adopt a fighting spirit.

___ **8.** Cancer patients who are in programs that help them develop a fighting spirit live longer than patients who are not in such programs.

___ **9.** People who witness or experience a horrific event, such as a bomb blast, may suffer from post-traumatic stress disorder and may start shaking uncontrollably and be startled when they hear sudden noises.

B Discuss your answers with a partner. Go back to the reading "Stress and Illness" and point to the language in the text that influenced your answers.

4 The Academic Word List Ⓥ

In academic writing and speech, certain words are used more frequently than in general writing and speech. Studies have shown that some of these words appear in academic language regardless of the academic subject matter. One researcher, Averil Coxhead of the University of Wellington, New Zealand, has created a list of these words, called the Academic Word List.

A Match an Academic Word List word from the text with a word or phrase of similar meaning in the right column.

___ **1.** encountered (Line 3)   **a.** very important

___ **2.** thereby (Line 8)   **b.** made smaller

___ **3.** major (Line 14)   **c.** seemingly

___ **4.** induced (Line 16)   **d.** in this way

___ **5.** apparently (Line 44)   **e.** showed

___ **6.** minimized (Line 46)   **f.** fall

___ **7.** demonstrated (Line 50)   **g.** made to happen

___ **8.** duration (Line 55)   **h.** met

___ **9.** data (Line 71)   **i.** information

___**10.** decline (Line 74)   **j.** length of time

B Use eight of the words from the Academic Word List above to complete the following short text.

Stress comes about when a _____ change takes place
                                   1
in a person's life. _____ from research suggest that when the
                         2
_____ of the stress is long and the stress is _____
        3   4
continually, then the chance of developing an illness is high. Several experiments
have _____ that the immune system reacts to stress. This reaction
               5
_____ causes a _____ in the immune system's
        6   7
effectiveness. However, there are also indications that the effects of stress can be
_____ if people react to stress in an active way.
        8

Chapter 1 Academic Vocabulary Review

The following are some of the words that appear in Chapter 1. They all come from the Academic Word List, a list of words that researchers have discovered occur frequently in many different types of academic texts. If you can learn these words, it should help you when you have a reading in almost any academic discipline. For a complete list of all the Academic Word List words in this chapter and in all the other readings in this book, see the Appendix on pages 213–214.

Reading 1 What Is Stress?	Reading 2 Coping with Stress	Reading 3 Stress and Illness
adapt	anticipate	apparently
collapse (n)	beneficial	conduct (v)
elements	commit	denial
encounter (v)	consequences	expose
predominantly	furthermore	link (n)
vary	schedule (v)	range (v)

Complete the following sentences with words from the lists above.

1. You should try to _____ a stressful event. It can help you cope with it.
2. The researcher decided to _____ an experiment to see if divorced people tended to get more illnesses than married people.
3. Some people try not to _____ themselves to stressors, but it is almost impossible to avoid them totally.
4. _____ it is a good thing to try to take control of stressful situations. That is what the research seems to suggest.
5. What are the _____ of getting too little exercise?
6. Different people react differently when they _____ a stressful event.
7. If you think you have a serious illness, you should _____ an appointment with a doctor as soon as possible.
8. After her divorce, she went through a period of physical and mental _____ .
9. The _____ between ultraviolet light and skin cancer is well known.
10. It is a good idea to _____ your diet. Eat something different at every meal.
11. Few things are as _____ as getting a good night's sleep every night.
12. A useful personality quality to have is the ability to _____ to new situations.

Developing Writing Skills

In this section, you will learn about the parts of an essay and do some short writing assignments that will help you organize a standard academic essay. At the end of the unit, you will be given your essay assignment and have the opportunity to apply this information.

The Parts of an Essay

A standard academic essay should have the following parts: an introduction, a body, and a conclusion. Depending on the instructor's assignment, each of these can be one or more paragraphs. A five-paragraph essay would typically have a one-paragraph introduction, a three-paragraph body, and a one-paragraph conclusion.

The most important element in an essay is the thesis statement, which usually occurs at the end of the introduction. The thesis statement contains the writer's main idea (his or her thesis). The thesis statement can often help the reader preview the organization of the essay by mentioning the topics that will be in the essay and by mentioning them in the order that they will occur.

Following the thesis statement are the body paragraphs that contain arguments or facts that support the thesis. Body paragraphs often begin with topic sentences that connect back to the thesis statement and look forward to the details in the rest of the paragraph.

Look at the following diagram and see how the thesis statement can provide a structure for the complete essay.

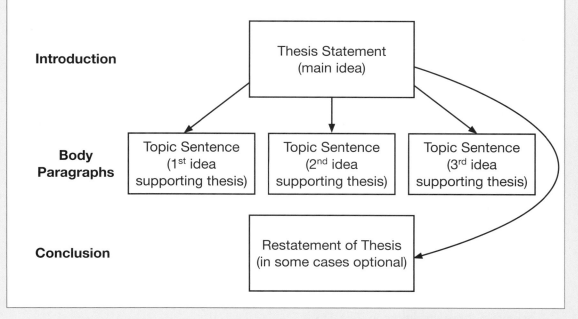

Introduction — Thesis Statement (main idea)

Body Paragraphs — Topic Sentence (1st idea supporting thesis) · Topic Sentence (2nd idea supporting thesis) · Topic Sentence (3rd idea supporting thesis)

Conclusion — Restatement of Thesis (in some cases optional)

A Read the following sentences from an essay on the stress of being a first-year university student. Place the letters *a–e* in the diagram below, depending on where you think the sentences belong in the essay.

a. The types of assignments in college and the standards of grading are typically very different from those in high school.

b. Clearly, there are many stressors for the young student during their first year of study at a university, especially when it is far from their hometown and friends.

c. Being away from home, building a new social life, and learning a new way of studying make the first year of college a particularly stressful time.

d. Some students adjust very quickly to being away from home, but for others this is not so easy.

e. Even though students today can stay in touch with their friends through social media, they still often experience intense loneliness when they first start college.

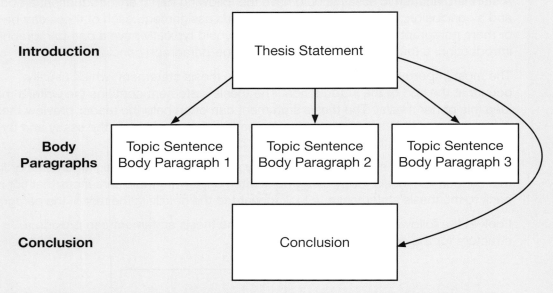

B Write a thesis statement that matches each of the following three topic sentences:

• The financial difficulties that occur after divorce are often very severe.

• Another major cause of stress during a divorce is loss of friends.

• For those who have to separate from their children, not seeing their children every day is extremely stressful.

C Write three topic sentences to start three body paragraphs that expand on the following thesis statement:

Therefore, it would seem that students going to college for the first time should try to predict what stressors they will experience, actively do things to reduce those stressors, and find ways to strengthen their personalities.

D Write a thesis statement, three topic sentences, and the opening of a conclusion for an essay on three stressors in your life.

Chapter 2
Lifestyle and Health

1 Personalizing the topic ®

> Thinking about your personal connections to a topic before you read about it will help you absorb new information on that topic.

Fill out this questionnaire. After you read the text, look at your answers to see if you are at risk for heart disease.

Are you at risk?	YES	NO
1. Are you male?	☐	☐
2. Do you smoke?	☐	☐
3. Are you overweight?	☐	☐
4. Does/did your mother or father have heart disease?	☐	☐
5. Are you a competitive person?	☐	☐
6. Do you often feel you don't have time to do what you want to do?	☐	☐
7. Do you often hide what you are really feeling?	☐	☐
8. Do you easily get angry?	☐	☐

2 Skimming ®

> *Skimming* means reading only small parts of text, such as the beginnings and ends of paragraphs, in order to get an overview of its organization. Skimming a text is an excellent prereading habit. When you do a close reading of the text after skimming it, you will find you read more fluently and accurately.

Skim through the text and find the paragraph that discusses each of the following topics. Write the number of the paragraph in the blank.

____ 1. Causes of heart disease

____ 2. Programs to help Type A personalities relax more

____ 3. Differences between Type A and Type B personalities

____ 4. Trends in heart disease within the United States and elsewhere in the world

____ 5. Reasons why Type A personalities are more susceptible to heart disease

____ 6. Differences in heart disease rates for men and women

Reading 1

HEART DISEASE

Heart disease is Western society's number-one killer. It is the leading cause of death for both men and women, and accounts for more than one in four of all deaths in America. Heart disease used to be considered a male disease, and among the middle aged this is still true.
5 However, since 1984, more women than men actually die from heart disease in the United States each year. It is just that the onset of heart disease starts later in women than in men. Some good news, though, for both genders is that deaths from heart disease in the United States

Fig. 2.1 Mortality rates from cardiovascular disease for men and women 1979–2006

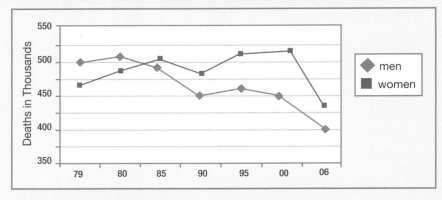

Source: American Heart Association

have been falling since the beginning of the twenty-first century (see
10 Figure. 2.1). Worldwide, however, the picture is not so good. Heart disease rates are climbing rapidly all around the globe as more and more cultures adopt a Western lifestyle – smoking more, exercising less, and eating a diet higher in fats.

Heart disease usually involves the formation of a fatty substance called *plaque* in the walls of the coronary arteries, which supply blood to the heart. If the arteries become narrowed enough or blocked, the person may suffer a heart attack (death of a region of heart muscle tissue). Among the many factors that have been found to be related to the risk of developing heart disease are high blood pressure (or *hypertension*), a history of heart disease among one's close relatives (indicating a possible genetic predisposition to the disease), cigarette smoking, being relatively overweight, and a high level of a fatty substance called *cholesterol* in the blood. In addition to all of these well-established risk factors, it is now clear that stress can have a major impact on the development of heart disease. People who continually undergo a great deal of stress – and who lack the ability to control it – are at a significantly greater risk for heart disease than people who undergo less stress or who can manage stress successfully. Jobs that impose high psychological demands but that provide the worker with little control – such as a cook, a waiter, or a hospital orderly – seem to breed heart disease.

The Type A behavior pattern

Whereas some jobs may make heavier psychological demands than others, certain sorts of people, regardless of their occupation, seem to make heavy psychological demands on themselves – and, as a result, run a greater risk of heart disease. People with a particular personality style, called the *coronary-prone behavior pattern* and commonly labeled **Type A**, have been found to be especially susceptible to heart disease. Type A people are hard-driving, competitive, and aggressive. They experience great time urgency, always trying to do more and more in less and less time. People who have an opposite sort of personality are termed **Type B**. Others are categorized somewhere in between.

Many studies have confirmed that Type A people are more susceptible to heart disease than Type B people. One probable reason is that Type A people tend to make greater demands on themselves and to expose themselves to more stressful situations than do Type B people. One study of college football players found, for example, that Type A players were rated by their coaches as playing harder than Type B players when they were injured. Type A people also tend to have an unusually intense physiological reaction to the stress that they encounter. When they are faced with a challenging situation, they tend to manifest higher blood pressure and greater increases in heart rate and in the level of epinephrine in their blood than Type B people. Some researchers believe that this greater physiological reactivity under stress – sometimes called *hot reactivity* – is the key to the link between the Type A pattern and heart disease.

Type A used to describe a personality that is hard-driving, competitive, and aggressive

Type B used to describe a personality that is easy-going, non-competitive, and unaggressive

The Type A personality finds it difficult to relax.

Women may reduce their risk of heart disease by talking openly about their emotions.

The bulk of the research on psychological factors in heart disease has focused on men rather than women. Even among women who face highly stressful situations, whether at work or at home, the risk
60 of heart disease remains considerably lower than for men. Many biological and psychological factors may contribute to this difference. Among them is the consistent finding that although women tend to express their emotions more openly than men do, their physiological reactions to stress tend to be less intense. In terms of the risk of heart
65 disease, then, it may be better to let one's emotions show outwardly than to bury them inside, where they may eventually cause damage to one's body.

Because of the links between the Type A behavior pattern and heart disease, various approaches have been taken to changing this
70 pattern of behavior. For example, Type A people have been taught relaxation exercises and other techniques to manage stress. They have been encouraged to develop nonstressful hobbies and they have been given therapy sessions to help change their pressured view of the world. Some programs have had a degree of success in altering
75 the behavioral and psychological reaction of Type A individuals. So far, however, the success has been limited. The Type A pattern seems to be learned over the course of many years, and it is supported by the competitive, achievement-oriented aspects of Western society. As such, it is not a simple matter to change this pattern. Indeed, as Joan
80 Borysenko notes, "One of the most stressful things for a Type A is to be told to relax."

1 Answering true/false questions Ⓐ Ⓡ

> True/false questions are fairly common in college tests. Read this list of strategies for answering them.
>
> - Answer every question. You always have a 50/50 chance of being right.
> - Pay special attention to statements with negatives in them. These are often tricky to answer. Remember that a negative statement that is correct is true.
> - Pay attention to words like *always* or *never* or *all*. Statements that are very "black or white" tend to be false. On the other hand, more tentative "gray" statements are more likely to be true.
> - Read all parts of a statement carefully. Some parts may be true, but if any one part of it is false, then the whole statement is false.
>
> In any series of true/false questions, there is usually about the same number of true statements as false ones.

Decide if the following statements are true (*T*) or false (*F*), according to the information in the reading.

____ **1.** More than 25 percent of all deaths in the United States are from heart disease.

____ **2.** Around the world, the numbers of people suffering from heart disease have been declining steadily.

____ **3.** If your close relatives have had heart disease, this is a possible indication that you may eventually suffer from heart disease.

____ **4.** Research has established that for some people there is a relationship between the degree of stress in their lives and the risk of developing heart disease.

____ **5.** Two men doing exactly the same job are equally likely to develop heart disease.

____ **6.** Type A people tend to have aggressive and unrelaxed personalities; however, they are better able to manage stress effectively and are less likely to develop heart disease than Type B people.

____ **7.** Only one researcher has ever found that Type A people are more susceptible to heart disease than Type B people.

____ **8.** When Type A people experience stress, they tend to have a higher heart rate and higher blood pressure than Type B people.

____ **9.** When a Type A man and a Type A woman do the same job and receive the same amount of stress, they have an equal chance of developing heart disease.

____ **10.** Most programs trying to change the behavior of Type A people have not been very successful.

2 Comparing Ⓦ

In this text, a number of comparisons are made. For example, Type A people are compared to Type B people, and men are compared to women. These comparisons can be made by using comparative adjectives, which can occur in the following structures:

ADJ + -er + than (used with adjectives of one syllable)

more + ADJ + than (used with adjectives of three syllables or more[1])

less + ADJ + than (used with most adjectives)

not as + ADJ + as (used with any adjective)

A For each adjective, write two sentences comparing Type A and Type B people. Start your first sentence by referring to Type A people and the second by referring to Type B people. The first one is done for you.

1. aggressive

   Type A people are more aggressive than Type B people.
   Type B people are less aggressive than Type A people.
   (or *Type B people are not as aggressive as Type A people.*)

2. competitive

3. laid-back

4. good at controlling their emotions

5. achievement-oriented

6. calm

B Many of the comparisons made in this text involve this structure:

   comparative adjective + noun + *than*

Make comparisons between Type A and Type B people in terms of each of the categories listed. In each case, refer to Type A people first in the sentence.

1. the psychological demands they make upon themselves

   Type A people make greater psychological demands upon themselves than Type B people.

2. their risk of having high blood pressure

3. their heart disease rate

4. their sense of time urgency

5. their reaction to difficult situations

---

[1] Two-syllable adjectives may act like one-syllable adjectives, for example, *happy/happier*; or like three-syllable adjectives, for example, *useful/more useful*.

1 Thinking about the topic ®

Work with a partner and discuss the following topics.

1. In what ways is smoking bad for the health of a smoker?

2. Is smoking common in your country? Do more men or more women smoke?

3. What, if anything, is the government in your country doing to encourage people not to smoke?

4. At what age do people start smoking? Why do they start?

5. The author states that addiction to smoking is "partly physiological" and also that people become "psychologically dependent on smoking." What is the difference?

6. What are some ways that people try to help them quit smoking?

2 Increasing reading speed ®

In college, you are often given very large reading assignments. You may have little time to read these slowly and carefully, so you need to develop ways to read quickly, but still retain the most important information. A good goal for a college reader is 250 words per minute with 70 percent comprehension. To practice increasing your reading speed, use the following techniques:

- Do not vocalize; that is, don't say the words under your breath as you read.
- Do not run your finger or a pencil beneath the words as you read.
- Try to focus on groups of words, not individual words.
- Try not to backtrack over the text.
- Guess at the general meaning of words you are not sure about.
- Skip over words that you have no idea about and that do not seem too important.
- Slow down slightly for key information, such as definitions and main ideas.
- Speed up for less important information, such as examples and unimportant details.

Read the text "Smoking" to practice reading for speed. (Do not at this time read the boxed text "Cigarette Pack Warnings.") Time yourself. When you finish, turn to the tasks that begin on page 39, and write down how long it took you to read the text.

Reading 2

SMOKING

The risks of smoking

The risks of smoking are hardly a well-guarded secret. The "Smoking Can Be Harmful to Your Health" warning is on every pack of cigarettes sold in the United States, and 97 percent of adults and teens agree that smoking is associated with lung cancer. Nearly as many people
5 also acknowledge smoking's links with other respiratory ailments and heart disease. A teen-to-the-grave smoker has a 50 percent chance of dying from the habit. According to the World Health Organization (WHO), the death rate from smoking will soon grow to 10 million people in the world every year, meaning that half a billion people alive
10 today will be killed by tobacco. Eliminating smoking would increase life expectancy worldwide more than any other preventive measure. It is no wonder then that, because smoking is generally viewed as the most important behavioral risk to health, it has become a central concern of health psychologists.

Why do people start smoking?

15 Smoking is a *pediatric* disease. It usually begins during early adolescence. It is especially common among those who get low grades at school, who drop out of school, who feel less in control of their future, and whose friends, parents, and siblings smoke.

We learn behaviors through the models we imitate and the
20 social rewards we receive. Adolescents are self-conscious and often think the world is watching their every move. So, they may begin smoking to imitate cool models, to get the social rewards of being accepted by other smokers, and to project a mature image. Typically, teens who start smoking have friends
25 who smoke and suggest its pleasures, and who offer them cigarettes. Among teens whose parents and best friends are nonsmokers, the rate is close to zero.

Why do people not stop smoking?

Once addicted to nicotine, we find it very difficult to stop. Tobacco products are as addictive as heroin or cocaine. Studies in Britain
30 and the United States show that at least one in three of those who try cigarettes become hooked. This addiction to smoking is partly physiological; smokers become used to the effects of nicotine and experience painful withdrawal symptoms when they give it up. In addition, people become psychologically dependent on smoking
35 as a way of reducing anxiety and coping with particular situations. Because of these physiological and psychological forces, quitting is difficult and the **relapse rate** is high.

relapse rate the rate at which people fall back to a previous state of illness or negative behavior

Helping smokers quit

Psychologists have helped develop a variety of behavior modification techniques to get people to stop smoking. These efforts include public warnings, counseling, drug treatments, hypnosis, aversive conditioning (e.g., making people smoke cigarette after cigarette until they feel sick), and support groups. The good news is that these treatments are often effective. The bad news is that all but one-fifth of the participants eventually succumb to the habit again. For those trying to quit by themselves, that is without group support, the odds are even lower.

Better news comes from the Centers for Disease Control (CDC) which reports that half of Americans who have ever smoked do manage to quit eventually after repeated attempts. Because so many people have stopped or not started smoking, the percentage of American, Canadian, and British smokers has dropped sharply over the last 30 years (see Figure 2.2). The drop has been most pronounced in these countries in the male smoking rate, which now barely exceeds that of women. Thanks in part to such trends, the death rate due to coronary heart disease in these countries has declined by about 30 percent since the mid-1960s. Smoking-related cancer deaths have also been declining, especially among men.

However, despite declining cigarette sales among educated Western adults, per capita cigarette consumption is near an all-time high worldwide. Smoking has skyrocketed in Asia. In China, where most men, but no more than 1 in 10 women, smoke, cigarette consumption soared from 100 billion cigarettes a year in the early 1950s to 1.6 trillion at the century's end. In Japan, 35 percent (50 percent of men) are smokers. Today, cigarette companies are targeting developing countries, such as Kenya and Zimbabwe, where rates of cigarette consumption have been historically low. The WHO therefore has predicted that in the next three decades, 70 percent of tobacco-related deaths will occur in developing countries, where people tend to be less aware of the dangers of smoking.

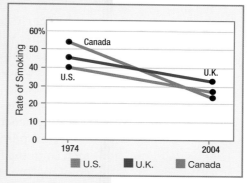

Fig. 2.2 Percentage of people who smoke in Canada, the U.S., and the U.K., 1974–2004

Source: Gallup.com

Preventing smoking

It is vastly easier to begin smoking than, once addicted, to stop. Social and psychological analyses of why adolescents start smoking have helped generate educational programs that teachers can implement easily and inexpensively. According to the National Cancer Institute, the key ingredients of such programs are:

- Information about the effects of smoking
- Information about peer, parent, and media influences
- Training in refusal skills, through modeling and role-playing

The informational ingredients can also be offered through mass media. In 1998, Florida initiated a massive youth-oriented media campaign to reduce the allure of smoking, and by early 1999, the number of 12- to 14-year-olds who reported smoking had dropped by 19 percent from the previous year.

There is another way to discourage smoking: Make it more immediately costly. The most effective rewards and punishments are immediate. When the delayed rewards of exercise compete with the immediate discomfort of doing so, the immediate consequences win out. Likewise, even knowing that in the long run smoking is often suicidal behavior, many continue to smoke. If we could only raise the immediate costs, consumption would surely go down. This is, in fact, what happened when the price of cigarettes in the United States went up by 70 percent between 1997 and 2001. Following this increase, teen smoking began declining, especially in states that also had strong smoking-prevention programs.

Cigarette Pack Warnings

In 1964, Canada was the first country in the world to require that a warning label appear on every cigarette pack sold. Since that time, most countries in the world have done the same. The first warnings were very mild. In English-speaking countries, they contained statements claiming that "cigarettes *may* be dangerous to your health" or "nicotine *may* cause lung cancer." These early warning labels had little effect and, as more evidence of the dangers of smoking became apparent, the labels became stronger: Cigarettes will kill you.

However, these warnings were still not particularly effective, especially in deterring young teenage smokers. In fact, some psychologists conducted studies that showed that the labels on cigarette pack actually triggered a response in teenagers to want to smoke.

So the next step taken in several countries was to add a very graphic picture on the pack. These packs often contain horribly frightening pictures of black lungs, dying babies, and diseased mouths with no teeth. In countries like Brazil and Canada, the pictures must take up 50 percent of the space on the pack. Research now shows that a large, graphic picture plus a strong verbal warning does have a deterrent effect. In 2010, the U.S. government finally agreed to require graphic images on cigarette packs in an attempt to bring national smoking levels down from 21 percent of the population to 12 percent by 2020.

1 Comprehension after speed reading ®

On Line a, write the time it took you to read the text in minutes or fractions of a minute (e.g., 7.2 minutes). Divide the number of words by the number of minutes and write the answer on Line c. This is your words per minute reading speed for this reading.

a. time to read in minutes   _____

b. number of words   __950__

c. wpm (b/a)   _____

d. number correct   _____

e. percent correct (dx10)   _____

Now test your understanding of this text while reading at speed by answering these multiple-choice comprehension questions without looking back at the text. Choose the best answer from the choices listed. Have your teacher check your answers and then fill in Lines d and e above. If you are reading at speed, a good goal is to get 70 percent of your answers correct. If you get 100 percent correct, you are either a genius or reading too carefully!

1. _____ people agree that smoking is associated with lung cancer.
   a. A few
   b. Most
   c. Almost all

2. When do people usually start smoking?
   a. when they are young adults (e.g., ages 20–29)
   b. when they are older teens (e.g., ages 17–19)
   c. when they are young teens (e.g., ages 13–15)

3. Why do people usually start smoking?
   a. to be accepted by their friends
   b. to be different from their friends
   c. to make their parents angry

4. Why is it difficult to quit smoking?
   a. Nicotine in cigarettes is highly addictive.
   b. People keep offering smokers cigarettes.
   c. Smoking gives smokers so much pleasure.

5. Which of the following is not a behavior modification technique that health psychologists have used to help smokers quit smoking?
   a. getting people to smoke one cigarette after another till they feel sick
   b. offering people money if they will stop smoking
   c. having people talk in support groups

6. Approximately _____ of smokers who manage to quit smoking start again.
   a. 80 percent
   b. 50 percent
   c. 20 percent

7. In which of the following countries has the number of people who smoke decreased greatly?
   a. United States and Japan
   b. Canada and Britain
   c. China and Zimbabwe

8. In which of the following countries has the number of people who smoke increased greatly?
   a. United States and Canada
   b. Asian countries, including China
   c. Kenya and Zimbabwe

9. Which of the following is *not* mentioned in this reading as an effective way to help smokers stop smoking?
   a. Provide them with information about the dangers of smoking.
   b. Put frightening pictures and warnings on cigarette packs.
   c. Get smokers to role-play refusing cigarettes.

10. An effective way to get people to stop smoking is to _____ .
   a. greatly raise the price of cigarettes
   b. put warnings on every pack of cigarettes
   c. tell smokers that smoking is going to kill them

2 Scanning ®

When you scan a text, you are usually looking for a very specific piece of information – often a date, a number, a percentage, a place or a person.

Scan the text including the boxed text "Cigarette Pack Warnings" on page 38 as quickly as possible to find the following:

1. The number of people that the WHO predicts will die every year in the world from smoking
2. The percentage of adult males who smoke in Japan
3. The place in the United States where a smoking campaign for teens was successful
4. The years when cigarette consumption in China was 100 billion a year
5. Three countries where cigarette smoking has decreased in the last 30 years
6. A country where the majority of men smoke
7. The percentage increase in the price of cigarettes between 1997 and 2001 in the United States
8. The year that cigarette warning labels first appeared on cigarette packets
9. The percentage of space a picture must occupy on a cigarette packet in Canada and Brazil

3 Describing change Ⓥ

In academic text, you will frequently find information about change. It is therefore helpful for you to learn specific words and phrases that writers use to express change.

A Complete the chart with the words below. Put them in the correct column, depending on whether they describe an upward (↑) or a downward (↓) change. If you need to look back at the words in the text, the paragraph numbers are given next to the words.

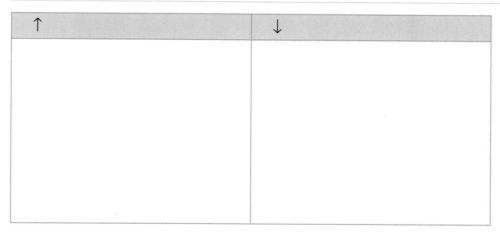

| grow to (1) | increase (1) | drop (6) | decline (6, 7) | skyrocket (7) |
| soar (7) | reduce (4, 9) | raise (10) | go down (10) | go up (10) |

↑	↓

B Complete the sentences below with the same verb that was used in the text to describe the change. Change the verb depending on the tense needed in the sentence.

1. Between 1997 and 2001, cigarette taxes in the United States _____ .

2. A campaign in Florida in the 1990s successfully _____ the allure of smoking for young people.

3. Cigarette consumption in China between 1950 and 1999 _____ .

4. The death rate due to coronary heart disease in the United States, Canada, and Britain _____ in the last 30 years.

5. Smoking in Asia _____ in the last few decades.

6. The percentage of people who smoke in the United States, Canada, and Britain _____ sharply.

7. If more people were to quit smoking, life expectancy around the world would _____ .

8. Male rates of cancer in countries where a large percentage of people have quit smoking _____ .

9. If cigarettes were to cost a lot more, it is quite likely that cigarette consumption would _____ .

4 Thinking critically ®

The purpose of reading is not just to gain new information, but to stimulate you to think critically. By reflecting on what you read, you can get ideas that are not directly stated by the writer, but that are suggested by the text.

Skim through the text again, including the boxed reading "Cigarette Pack Warnings." In groups, discuss why psychologists might find smoking to be an interesting subject for them to study. Then make a list of different aspects of smoking that psychologists might research.

1 Thinking about the topic ®

Discuss the answers to the following questions with a partner.

1. What fitness activities are popular in your country? Are there health clubs? Do people work out on machines? Is bodybuilding popular? Is jogging popular?

2. What are some of the benefits of regular exercise?

3. Are many people very religious in your country? What do religious people do and not do compared to nonreligious people?

4. Many studies seem to suggest that highly religious people live longer than nonreligious people. How do you think this could be explained?

2 Scientific terms ® V

When you are reading scientific literature, you need to be aware of important scientific terms and how they are expressed in English. One basic term is *correlation*. A correlation tells if two factors (often called *variables*) are related. When scientists find a correlation, they try to account for, or explain, it. To do this they have to control for variables that might affect the results.

A Read these sentences from Paragraph 3. Then answer the questions that follow.

"In one experiment, researchers randomly assigned one-third of mildly depressed female college students to a program of aerobic exercise and another third to a treatment of relaxation exercises; the remaining third – the control group – received no treatment."

1. What does it mean that the researchers *randomly assigned* students to groups?

2. What is a *control group*? What does "treatment" mean in this context?

3. What were the scientists trying to test?

B Read these sentences from Paragraph 8. Then answer the questions that follow.

"More than 1,000 studies have sought to correlate the faith factor with health. A . . . survey in 1999 followed 21,104 people over eight years. After controlling for age, sex, race, and religion, researchers found that non-attendees of religious services were 1.87 times more likely to have died than those attending more than weekly."

1. Explain the 1999 study in your own words.

2. What factors had *a* high correlation? What variables did researchers control for? How do you think they did this?

Reading 3

HEALTHFUL BEHAVIOR

Fig. 2.3 Effects of exercise on the depression score of mildly depressed college women

In this section, we study two very different approaches to managing stress and thus creating the conditions for greater healthfulness: exercise and spirituality.

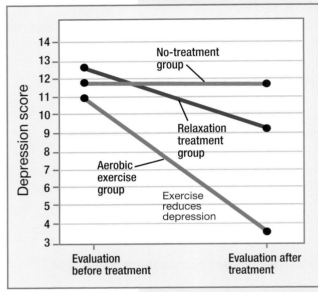

Primary Source:
McCann, I.L., & Holmes, D.S.

Exercise

Many studies suggest that aerobic 5 exercise, that is, exercise that increases heart and lung fitness, such as jogging, swimming, and biking, can reduce stress, depression, and anxiety. In a 2002 survey, for example, non-exercisers were 10 twice as likely as exercisers to report being "not too happy." But if we state this observation the other way around – that stressed and depressed people exercise less – cause and effect become unclear.

15   Experiments have resolved this ambiguity. In one experiment, researchers randomly assigned one-third of mildly depressed female college students to a program of aerobic 20 exercise and another third to a treatment of relaxation exercises; the remaining third – the control group – received no treatment. As Figure 2.3 shows, 10 weeks later, the women in the aerobic exercise group reported the greatest decrease in depression.

More than 150 other studies confirm that exercise reduces 25 depression and anxiety and can therefore be a useful addition to treatment that includes antidepressant drugs and psychotherapy. In fact, some research suggests that exercise is better than drugs in preventing symptom recurrence.

Researchers are now wondering why aerobic exercise alleviates 30 negative emotions. Researchers know that exercise releases certain chemicals in the body's bloodstream that can affect emotions. However, they also wonder whether the benefits of exercise are a side effect of the sound sleep that people experience after exercise, or perhaps a sense of accomplishment or the fact that one's improved 35 physique may influence one's emotional state and self-esteem.

Research certainly reveals that exercise not only boosts our mood, but also strengthens the heart, increases blood flow, keeps blood vessels open, and lowers both blood pressure and the blood pressure

reaction to stress. Compared with inactive adults, people who exercise
40 suffer half as many heart attacks. One study that followed Finnish
twins for nearly 20 years showed that occasional exercise reduced the
risk of death by 29 percent compared with no exercise. Daily exercise
reduced death risk by 43 percent. By one estimate, moderate exercise
adds two years to one's expected life.

Spirituality

45 Throughout history, religion and medicine have joined forces
in caring for the sick. Hospitals, which were first established in
monasteries, often carried the names of saints. However, as medical
science matured, healing and religion diverged. Rather than asking
God to heal their sick children from smallpox, people were able to
50 vaccinate them. Rather than seeking a spiritual healer when burning
with a fever, people were able to use antibiotics. Recently, however,
religion and healing have been converging once again.

- Of the United States' 135 medical schools, 101 offered spirituality and
health courses in 2005, up from five in 1992.
55 - Since 1995, Harvard Medical School has annually attracted 1,000 to
2,000 health professionals to its Spirituality and Healing in Medicine
conferences.
- Duke University has established a Center for Spirituality, Theology,
and Health.
60 - A survey found that 99 percent of U.S. family physicians agreed that
"personal prayer, meditation, or other spiritual practices" can enhance
medical treatment.

Is there fire underneath all this smoke? More than 1,000
studies have sought to correlate the faith factor with health.
65 A U.S. National Health Interview survey in 1999 followed
21,104 people over eight years. After controlling for age, sex,
race, and religion, researchers found that non-attendees of
religious services were 1.87 times more likely to have died
than those attending more than weekly. This translated into
70 a life expectancy at age 20 of 83 years for frequent attendees
and 75 years for infrequent attendees (see Figure 2.4).

These findings indicate that, as a predictor of health and
longevity, religious involvement rivals nonsmoking and
exercise effects. Such findings demand explanation. Can
75 you imagine what might account for the correlation?

Consider one obvious possibility: Women are more
religiously active than men, and women outlive men. So

Fig. 2.4 Religious
attendance and life
expectancy

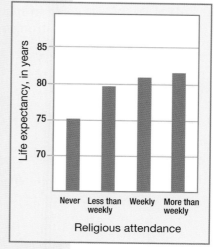

Primary Source: U.S.
Centers for Disease
Control

perhaps religious involvement is merely an expression of the gender effect on longevity.

80   Second, religiously active people have healthier lifestyles; for example, they smoke and drink less. Third, social support is another variable that may help explain the faith factor. For all the major organized religions in the world, faith is not solo spirituality, but a communal experience. Support networks exist for people when 85 misfortune strikes. Finally, in many very religious communities, divorce, which is highly stressful, is almost nonexistent.

    But even after controlling for gender, unhealthful behaviors, social ties, and divorce, the mortality studies find much of the mortality reduction remaining. Researchers therefore speculate that a set of 90 variables exist that may explain this. These variables include the well-being associated with a coherent worldview, a sense of hope for the long-term future, feelings of ultimate acceptance, and the relaxed meditation of prayer. These variables might also explain another recent finding among the religiously active: healthier immune 95 functioning and fewer hospital admissions.

    Although the religion-health correlation is yet to be fully explained, Harold Pincus, Deputy Medical Director of the American Psychiatry Association believes these findings "have made clear that anyone involved in providing health care services . . . cannot ignore 100 . . . the important connection between spirituality, religion, and health."

    Let's summarize the contents of this unit: Sustained emotional reactions to stressful events can lead to sickness. However, we can cope with stressors by problem solving or emotional coping. And we 105 can manage stress by making ourselves emotionally and physically stronger.

1 Reading for main ideas ⓡ

Remember that identifying the main ideas in a text is the most important task when you are reading.

Find the two main ideas of "Healthful Behavior" in the following statements.

1. Exercise seems to make people not only physically healthier, but also emotionally healthier.
2. Religious people tend to have fewer illnesses than nonreligious people.
3. People who exercise often look better and therefore often have more self-esteem.
4. Because religious people tend to be women, and women live longer than men, religious people tend to live longer lives than nonreligious people.
5. Research seems to suggest that having strong religious faith influences how healthy and long-living a person will be.
6. Exercising regularly can help you live a longer life and have fewer illnesses.
7. Religion and health have been connected for centuries.

2 Understanding paragraph structure ⓦ

Not only does an academic reading have one or two main ideas, but each paragraph in a reading should have a controlling idea that is supported by the details in the paragraph. Sometimes it is a good idea to identify key paragraphs and then outline them in note form.

A Look at this outline for Paragraph 5 (lines 29–35). Interpret the note-taking symbols.

> A. Possible explanations for why aerobic exercise → ↓↓ negative emotions
>   1. Exercise releases chemicals that affect emotions
>   2. Exercise → ↑ sleep → feeling better
>   3. Exercise → a sense of achievement
>   4. Exercise improves one's body → ↑ self-esteem

B Make a similar outline for Paragraph 9 (lines 63–71).

C Look at the structure of the topic sentence in Paragraph 5 and use the same structure to write a topic sentence for Paragraph 9.

3 Describing experimental results Ⓥ Ⓡ

When you are reading scientific literature, you will often read about the findings of an experiment or study. You should learn the meanings of the verbs that introduce the experimental results. Verbs such as *show*, *reveal*, *indicate*, and *confirm* have some small but important differences in meaning.

Consider the following language used in different parts of the reading "Healthful Behavior" and answer the questions that follow.

Many studies suggest . . .
Other studies confirm that . . .
One study showed that . . .
Studies have sought to correlate . . .
These findings indicate that . . .
Research reveals that . . .

1. What is the difference between a study that *suggests* something is true and a study that *shows* that something is true?
2. What is the difference between a study that *shows* that something is true and a study that *confirms* that something is true?
3. If studies *have sought to correlate* two things, do we know if the studies were successful or not?
4. What is the difference between *studies* and *findings*?
5. Which is stronger: when a finding *suggests* something or when it *indicates* something?
6. Which is stronger: when a finding *indicates* something or *shows* something?
7. Which verb phrase in the list above suggests that the results of the research were something that the researchers had not been looking for or were surprised by?

4 Preparing for a short-answer test Ⓐ Ⓦ

One of the best ways to prepare for a short-answer test is to write down questions that you think the professor will ask. Remember that your professor will probably ask different types of questions, not just questions that ask you to recall information (Type 1 questions).

Short-answer question types

Type 1: Questions about data

These are *what*, *when*, *how*, *where*, and *who* questions. They ask you to define, list, locate, identify, recall, describe, and so on.

Type 2: Questions that develop concepts from the data

These are questions that ask you to discuss the data, point to relationships between different parts of the data, compare and contrast, analyze, predict, and so on.

Type 3: Questions that call for critical judgment

These questions ask you to evaluate, rank, rate, or assess aspects of the data and justify your answers.

A Write four questions that you think a professor might ask about this text on a short-answer quiz. Use all three question types. Make sure you can answer the questions yourself!

B Exchange questions with a partner. Answer each other's questions orally and then tell your partner whether or not you think your questions were answered satisfactorily.

5 Writing short answers to test questions Ⓐ Ⓦ

In addition to practicing anticipating questions that will be on a test, it is useful to practice writing answers to them under time pressure.

A With your partner from Task 4, choose the two best questions that you thought of. Give yourselves a reasonable time limit and write answers to your questions.

B Read each other's answers and comment on how complete they are. Is any necessary information missing?

Chapter 2 Academic Vocabulary Review

The following are some of the words that appear in Chapter 2. They all come from the Academic Word List, a list of words that researchers have discovered occur frequently in many different types of academic texts. If you can learn these words, it should help you when you have a reading in almost any academic discipline. For a complete list of all the Academic Word List words in this chapter and in all the other readings in this book, see the Appendix on pages 213–214.

Reading 1 Heart Disease	Reading 2 Smoking	Reading 3 Healthful Behavior
alter	acknowledge	ambiguity
confirm	consumption	coherent
considerably	implement	network
intense	likewise	randomly
reactions	odds	seek
undergo	target	variables

Complete the following sentences with words from the lists above.

1. His _____ was to lose 40 pounds over the next six months.
2. The researcher _____ put people into three different groups.
3. People who attend religious services regularly often have a large _____ of friends.
4. He gets angry very easily, but he refuses to _____ that he has a problem.
5. What the president said was very clear. There was no _____ at all.
6. The _____ of too much fat in one's diet can lead to a buildup of cholesterol in the bloodstream.
7. You'll _____ withdrawal symptoms when you try to quit smoking.
8. Don't _____ anything. Everything is perfect just the way it is.
9. The _____ of dying from lung cancer are greatly increased if you smoke.
10. She experienced feelings of _____ happiness during the wedding service.
11. Your arguments just don't seem to be _____ to me. I'm having trouble seeing the logic in what you are saying.
12. You'll feel _____ better if you give up smoking, exercise more, and have a better diet.

Practicing Academic Writing

In Unit 1, you have learned about a variety of factors that influence physical and emotional health. Use this information to write an essay on the topic below.

Health Risk Factors

Think of someone you know or know about (e.g., a famous person, a relative, or a friend) who may have some health risks. Explain these risks, providing evidence from the readings. Consider which of these risks could be reduced or eliminated if the person made some changes in his or her life. Finally, explain how these changes could lead to a healthier life.

PREPARING TO WRITE

Making a list

Before you start writing, you need to gather some ideas. One way to get ideas is to make lists. You will not write about all of the ideas in your lists, but lists will give you topics to choose from. Also, as you write a list, new ideas and topics will come to you.

A Practice making and working with lists to assemble ideas.

B Make a list of three or four people about whom you could write your essay.

_____   _____

_____   _____

C Tell a classmate about these people. Talk about why you think they might provide good material for your essay. Have your classmate help you decide who might be the best person to write about, and why.

D After you have chosen the person you are going to write about, make two lists. In one list, write the stressors that this person suffers from (see Chapter 1, "What Is Stress?" and "Coping with Stress"). In the other list, write the behaviors the person has (see Chapter 2, "Heart Disease" and "Smoking").

Stressors   **Behaviors**

_____   _____

_____   _____

E For each item in your lists, go back to the readings in the unit and find evidence that each of these factors poses a health risk. Write one or two sentences that explain the risk factor according to the evidence in the reading.

Stressor example: My uncle is an airline pilot.

> People who have stressful jobs may get a number of different illnesses. For example, it is not unusual for people in stressful jobs to develop stomach ulcers.

Behavior example: My uncle gets angry very easily.

> According to the reading "Heart Disease," people who get angry very easily are more likely to develop heart disease than calmer people.

F You are also going to write about the lifestyle changes this person could adopt to help him or her stay healthy. You can get a lot of ideas about what to advise this person from the readings in this unit.

1. If the person you are writing about has a great number of stressors in his or her life, review the reading "Coping with Stress" on page 12. Make a list of behaviors this person could adopt to help cope with the stressors.

2. If the person has a hot-tempered personality, review the reading "Heart Disease" on page 30. Make a list of ways this person could try to live more calmly.

3. If the person smokes, go back to the reading "Smoking" on page 36. Make a list of ideas to try to help him or her give up smoking.

4. If the person does not exercise much or could include more spirituality in his or her life, review the reading "Healthful Behavior" on page 44. Make a list of behaviors for this person to try.

NOW WRITE

1 Writing first drafts

> Your first attempt at writing on a topic is a first draft. Very few people write a "perfect" first draft. A first draft gets some ideas, sentences, and paragraphs down on paper. You can then read through them and work out how to improve your writing.

A Review all the lists that you wrote in the Preparing to Write section on pages 51–52. Sort through the different ideas you could write about. Then formulate your thesis. (See The Parts of an Essay on pages 27–28 for a discussion about a thesis and thesis statements.)

B Write an introductory paragraph about the person who has risk factors. Tell your readers who this person is and briefly indicate the stressors in his or her life and his or her risky health behaviors.

C At the end of your introduction, write a thesis statement that prepares the reader for the body of your essay and the different ideas that you are going to include.

D Before you write your body paragraphs, read the following about how to structure body paragraphs and do a short exercise on topic sentences.

2 Structuring body paragraphs

The thesis statement in the introduction prepares the reader for the body paragraphs. In the same way, the topic sentence in a body paragraph prepares the reader for the rest of the paragraph. The topic sentence tells the reader what the topic of the paragraph is and what the writer wants to say about that topic. The rest of the paragraph is the support that "proves" to the reader that the topic sentence is accurate or true.

A Read the following three topic sentences. Work with a partner and explain to each other what information is likely to be in the rest of the paragraph – the support that provides evidence for the topic sentence.

- The two stressors that are most likely to cause my uncle to suffer an illness are his profession and his family situation.
- Two behavioral risk factors that can lead to major illnesses are lack of a calm personality and smoking.
- Clearly there are lifestyle and personality changes that my uncle could adopt that would help him lead a long and healthy life.

B Write body paragraphs about your chosen person. You could write about:

The stressors in his or her life

His or her unhealthful behaviors

Possible lifestyle changes he or she could make

C Use your introduction and body paragraphs to write your first draft.

Revising and editing

Once you have written a first draft, you can revise and edit it. Revising refers to the process of improving the content of the essay; editing refers to making the language of the essay accurate. By reading through your essay many times, you will find places to make changes and improvements. You should continue to do this until you feel the essay clearly, accurately, and effectively expresses your ideas.

A Read through your essay or ask a friend to read through it. You or your friend should look for things that are unclear, confusing, or unconvincing. Use your friend's feedback to help you revise.

B Answer the following questions to make sure that your essay has the parts of a standard academic essay. Make changes in your second draft if it doesn't.

1. *Did you include a thesis statement in your introductory paragraph?*
Check to see that you have a thesis statement that prepares the reader for the body of the essay.

2. *Did you include topic sentences in your body paragraphs?*
Check your body paragraphs to see if you have written a general opening statement that prepares the reader for your ideas in the rest of the paragraph.

3. *Did you support your topic sentences well?*
Check to see if you have enough details that make the reader feel that your topic sentences are true. If not, add more details to make your ideas more convincing.

4. *Did you write a conclusion to your essay?*
Check to see if you wrote a conclusion that reminds the reader of your thesis.

C Read through your essay to edit it.

1. Look back at Task 4, Parallel Sentence Structure, on page 9. Have you used parallel sentence structure in any of your paragraphs? Experiment with this use of language and attempt to use one or two examples of it in your essay.

2. Look back at Task 2, Hedging, on page 23. Are some of your statements too certain? Should you use some hedging language when there is not 100 percent certainty? Find places in your essay where it might be better to use language such as *might*, *can*, *possibly*, *it is likely that*, and so on.

3. Read through your essay now for possible spelling mistakes, punctuation errors, subject-verb agreement errors, and incorrect use of past tense and articles. Make corrections whenever you find errors.

Unit 2
Development Through Life

In this unit, you will look at stages of human development after childhood. In Chapter 3, you will read about adolescence, or the teen years, which can be a stressful period for some young people as they move toward adulthood. In Chapter 4, you will see how adult life can be divided into three stages and you will learn about the different challenges, problems, and joys of each.

Contents

In Unit 2, you will read and write about the following topics.

Chapter 3 The Teen Years	Chapter 4 Adulthood
Reading 1 Defining Adolescence	**Reading 1** Early Adulthood
Reading 2 Physical Change in Adolescence	**Reading 2** Middle Adulthood
Reading 3 Cognitive and Social Development in Adolescence	**Reading 3** Late Adulthood

Skills

In Unit 2, you will practice the following skills.

R Reading Skills

Personalizing the topic
Previewing art and graphics
Reading for main ideas
Skimming
Reading for details
Thinking critically
Reading actively
Thinking about the topic
Applying what you have read
Examining graphics
Increasing reading speed
Comprehension after speed reading
Describing change

W Writing Skills

Understanding paragraph structure
Understanding text structure
Hedging
Gerunds as subjects
Using data from a graphic
Journal writing
Paragraph topics
Paragraph main ideas
Supporting main ideas
Paraphrasing

V Vocabulary Skills

Word families
Synonyms
Collocations
Guessing meaning from context
Describing change

A Academic Success Skills

Definition answers on tests
The SQ3R system
Taking notes in the margins
Synthesizing
Group projects

Learning Outcomes

Write an essay comparing and contrasting two consecutive periods of life.

Previewing the Unit

Before reading a unit (or chapter) of a textbook, it is a good idea to preview the contents page and think about the topics that will be covered. This will give you an overview of how the unit is organized and what it is going to be about.

Read the contents page of Unit 2 on page 56 and do the following activities.

Chapter 3: The Teen Years

A Most of Chapter 3 deals with the period of life called *adolescence*. Discuss the following questions about when this period begins and ends.

1. What events mark the beginning of adolescence? In other words, when does childhood end?

2. What events mark the end of this period? In other words, when does early adulthood begin?

3. Based on your discussion of Questions 1 and 2, what age range would you give to adolescence?

B In many cultures, there is a stereotype of teenage behavior. Describe this behavior and discuss whether you think it is true that most teenagers act this way.

Chapter 4: Adulthood

A In Chapter 4, adulthood is divided into three periods. The first two are called *early adulthood, adulthood* and *middle adulthood*. Discuss the following questions.

1. What are some of the typical events in people's lives during these two periods of adulthood?

2. What ages do you typically associate with these periods? Fill in the box.

early adulthood: from ___ to ___ years old
middle adulthood: from ___ to ___ years old

B The last section of Chapter 4 addresses *late adulthood*. With a partner, discuss why you think this period of life may present a great challenge both for the elderly themselves and for their children.

Chapter 3
The Teen Years

1 Personalizing the topic ®

In the United States, there is a stereotype of the adolescent. This stereotype reveals someone who has many problems, is often rebellious, and does not communicate well with his or her parents.

To what extent is/was your adolescence like this? Respond to the following statements on a scale of 1–5. If you agree strongly, circle *1*; if you disagree strongly circle *5*. Compare your responses with a classmate's.

During my adolescence I was/have been . . .	Strongly agree		Neutral		Strongly disagree
a very rebellious	1	2	3	4	5
b often in conflict with my parents	1	2	3	4	5
c full of negative thoughts about life	1	2	3	4	5
d under a great deal of stress	1	2	3	4	5

2 Previewing art ®

You can often learn a lot about the content of a text simply by looking at the art and by reading the captions that accompany it.

Look at the three pieces of art that accompany this reading. Each piece shows young people in a different way. Work with a partner. Describe each piece of art and then say why you think these pieces of art were chosen to accompany the reading.

Reading 1

DEFINING ADOLESCENCE

The period of development that we call **adolescence** is an exciting one. It is filled with discovery, turmoil, growth toward independence, and the beginning of lifelong commitments. It is clearly a period of transition – from the dependence of childhood to the independence
5 of adulthood. It is very difficult, however, to specify exactly when adolescence begins or when it ends.

adolescence
a period of transition from childhood, often filled with turmoil

We may choose to define adolescence in biological terms. In that case, adolescence begins with the onset of puberty (with sexual maturity and a readiness to
10 reproduce) and ends with the end of physical growth. Or we may adopt a more psychological perspective. This approach emphasizes the development of the cognitions, feelings, and behaviors that characterize

The uncooperative teenager may, in fact, be more of a stereotype than a reality.

adolescence. Additionally, it is also possible to think about adolescence from a social perspective by examining the role of adolescents in society. Such views generally define adolescence in terms of being in-between – not yet an adult, but no longer a child. In this context, the period usually lasts from the early teen years through one's highest level of education, when the individual is thought to enter the adult world.

Actually, whether we accept a biological, psychological, or social approach to defining adolescence, we usually are talking about people between the ages of approximately 12 and 20. Some psychologists consider this a period of growth and positive change; others view adolescence as a period of great turmoil, stress, rebellion, and negativism.

Adolescence may very well be filled with conflict, storm, and stress, but it is also a period of adjustment that most of us manage to survive quite well. In fact, the picture of the troubled, rebellious, difficult, and uncooperative adolescent is probably more of a social stereotype than a reality.

As some children reach adolescence, they may start to be difficult and uncooperative.

1 Reading for main ideas Ⓡ

Skim the text. Which of the following best expresses the main idea?

1. There are three different ways in which it is possible to define adolescence.

2. The stereotype of the adolescent is that of a rebellious, negative, troubled young person.

3. Adolescence is an exciting period of life.

2 Understanding paragraph structure Ⓦ Ⓡ

Look at the structure of the second paragraph, which is given here in skeleton form, and then answer the questions.

> (sentence one). In that case, (sentence two). Or (sentence three). This approach (sentence four). Additionally, (sentence five). Such views (sentence six). In this context, (sentence seven).

1. The second paragraph describes three ways of looking at adolescence. What are they?

2. Which sentence or sentences discuss
   a. the first way? _____
   b. the second way? _____
   c. the third way? _____

3. Which words signal the transition from
   a. the first to the second way? _____
   b. the second to the third way? _____

4. Words like *this, that,* and *such* refer back to previous ideas in a paragraph. To what previous ideas do the following refer?
   a. In that case, . . . _____
   b. This approach . . . _____
   c. Such views . . . _____

5. We have read in The Parts of an Essay on page 27 that paragraphs typically have a topic sentence that expresses the main idea of the paragraph. Does Paragraph 2 have a topic sentence? If yes, which one is it? If no, write a suitable one.

3 Definition answers on tests Ⓐ Ⓡ

Often a test on an academic reading will include an item that asks you to define a key term. If the term has only one possible definition, you can begin your answer like this:

> X is . . .

If the term can be defined in different ways, here are some other common ways to introduce the definition of the term:

> X may be defined as . . .
> X can be defined in different ways . . .
> X is often defined as . . .

A Look back at the reading and your answers to the questions in Tasks 1 and 2. Then close your book and on a separate piece of paper write a one-paragraph answer to the following test item:

Define *adolescence*.

B Compare your answer with a partner's. Make sure you both have complete answers.

4 Word families Ⓥ Ⓡ

One way to build your academic vocabulary is to notice different forms of the same word. The words probably belong to the same word family and are probably related in meaning.

A Scan through the reading and find other word forms for the words in the left-hand column. Write the word that you find and check *adj.* (adjective), *v.* (verb), or *n.* (noun).

		adj.	v.	n.
1. specific (adj.)	specify	__	✓	__
2. commit (v.)		__	__	__
3. emphasis (n.)		__	__	__
4. mature (adj.)		__	__	__
5. cooperate (v.)		__	__	__
6. negative (adj.)		__	__	__

B Compare your answers with a partner's and check that you both know the meanings of both words in each answer.

1 Previewing art and graphics Ⓡ

Before reading a text, examine any graphs, diagrams, charts, photographs, or illustrations. You can quickly get a good introduction to the content of a text by looking at these visual displays.

Look at Figure 3.1 in the text and answer this question: What are three differences in the way girls and boys grow between the ages of one and 19?

1. _____
2. _____
3. _____

2 Skimming Ⓡ

Remember that when you skim, you do not have to read every word. You just need to be able to grasp the organization of a text and its main ideas.

A Skim through the text and write the number of the paragraph that addresses each of the following topics.

___ **a.** The effects of reaching puberty before most of your peers

___ **b.** The effects of maturing later than most of your peers

___ **c.** The psychological effects of sudden physical changes, such as one's growth spurt

___ **d.** The average ages and rates at which boys and girls increase in height

B Compare your answers with a partner's.

Reading 2

PHYSICAL CHANGE IN ADOLESCENCE

The onset of adolescence is generally marked by two biological or physical changes. First, there is a marked increase in height and weight, known as a **growth spurt**, and second, there is sexual maturation. Undergoing these changes may have a significant impact 5 on an individual's psychological well-being. Moreover, the impact varies considerably depending on whether one is a boy or a girl and whether the changes occur at either a very early or very late age compared to one's peers.

The growth spurt of early adolescence 10 usually occurs in girls at an earlier age than it does in boys. Girls begin their growth spurt as early as 9 or 10 years of age and then slow down at about age 15. Boys generally show their increased rate 15 of growth between the ages of 12 and 17 years. Indeed, males usually don't reach their adult height until their early 20s, whereas girls generally attain their maximum height by their late teens. 20 Figure 3.1 illustrates one way to represent the adolescent growth spurt in graphic form.

At least some of the potential psychological turmoil of early adolescence 25 may be a direct result of the growth spurt. It is not uncommon to find increases in weight and height occurring so rapidly that boys in particular have a hard time coordinating their larger hands and feet and may appear awkward 30 and clumsy. Boys also have the problem of voice change. As their vocal cords grow and lengthen, the pitch of the voice is lowered. Much to the embarrassment of many a teenage boy, this transition is seldom smooth, and the boy may suffer through weeks or months of a squeaking, crackling, and changing of pitch right in the middle of a 35 serious conversation.

growth spurt
a marked increase in height, typically occurring in adolescence

Fig. 3.1 Adolescent growth spurts of boys and girls

Source: Tanner, Whitehouse, and Takaishi

Many boys and girls reach puberty before or after most of their peers, or age mates, and are referred to as *early bloomers* or *late bloomers*. Reaching puberty well before or well after others of one's age does have some psychological effects, although few are long lasting. An early blooming girl will probably be taller, stronger, faster, and more athletic than other girls (and many of the boys). She is likely to start dating earlier and to marry at a younger age than her peers. Because of the premium put on physical activity in boys, the early maturing boy is at a great advantage. He will have more early dating experiences, which will raise his status with his peers.

For young teenagers of both sexes, being a late bloomer is more negative in its impact than being an early bloomer. There is some evidence that late-maturing boys carry a sense of inadequacy and poor self-esteem into adulthood. Some late-maturing girls, however, feel – at least in retrospect – that being a late bloomer was an advantage because it offered them an opportunity to develop some broad interests, rather than becoming "boy crazy" like so many of their peers in early adolescence. Although generalizations are dangerous, we may suggest that (1) early maturity is more advantageous than later maturity, and (2) boys profit from early maturity more than girls and may suffer more than girls from later maturity.

With all of the physical and physiological changes that occur in early adolescence, it is easy to see why G. Stanley Hall, in the first textbook written about adolescence, was moved to describe the period as one of "second birth" (Hall, 1905).

1 Reading for details ®

A According to the information in the reading, complete the chart below with the following phrases.

may feel inadequate as an adult
can have time to develop broad interests
is likely to have respect from peers

could be "boy crazy"
might start dating younger than most
might marry younger than most

An early-blooming girl	
A late-blooming girl	
An early-blooming boy	
A late-blooming boy	

B According to this reading, which is it better to be? Number the following choices in order of best (*1*) to worst (*4*).

___ **a.** an early-blooming girl

___ **b.** a late-blooming girl

___ **c.** an early-blooming boy

___ **d.** a late-blooming boy

2 Understanding text structure Ⓦ Ⓡ

Academic texts are sometimes written in standard essay format; that is, they have a beginning (an introduction), a middle (body paragraphs), and an end (a conclusion). A good introductory paragraph provides a road map for the content of the text and contains a thesis statement (see The Parts of an Essay on page 26). Good body paragraphs provide the evidence to support the thesis. A good concluding paragraph provides satisfactory closure to the text.

Reread the introductory and concluding paragraphs of "Physical Change in Adolescence" and then discuss the following questions with a partner.

1. In what ways does the introduction prepare the reader for the content of the body paragraphs? Which words and phrases tell you about the topics that are going to be in the reading?

2. Is there a thesis statement in the introductory paragraph? What is it? How do the body paragraphs provide evidence to show this statement is true?

3. Does the concluding paragraph provide good closure to the text? Why or why not?

3 Hedging W R

> Remember that hedging language allows a writer to write about what *usually*, *generally*, or *tends to* happen and about what *is likely to* happen or *may*, *might*, or *could* happen. It allows the writer to write about trends, not absolutes.

A The writer in this text warns that "generalizations are dangerous" because not all early or late-blooming boys and girls react in the same way. As a result, the writer uses many "hedges" while writing. There are at least 18 hedges in this text. Circle as many as you can find.

B Compare your answers with a partner's.

C Look back at page 65. Put the hedges that you found into the following categories:

Modals: _____

Phrases: _____

Adverbs: _____

Quantifiers: _____

4 Gerunds as subjects W

> A verb form of a word may sometimes be used as part of a noun phrase that acts as the subject of a sentence. Usually when this happens, the *-ing* form of the verb, or the gerund, is used.

A Underline the subjects and circle the main verbs in these sentences. The first one is done for you as an example.

1. Being a late bloomer (was) an advantage [for some late-maturing girls] . . . (Line 41)

2. Undergoing these changes [at either a very early age or at a very late age compared to one's peers] may have a significant impact on an individual's psychological well-being. (Lines 4–5)

3. Reaching puberty well before or well after others of one's age does have some psychological effects . . . (Line 29)

4. . . . being a late bloomer is more negative in its impact than being an early bloomer. (Lines 37–38)

B Complete the sentences below with ideas from the text. Use different examples of hedging language (see Task 3), if necessary.

1. Being a late bloomer _____ for a boy.

2. Reaching puberty early _____ for a girl.

3. Maturing late _____ for a girl.

4. Being an early bloomer _____ for a boy.

5 Personalizing the topic ®

> Relating new information to your own personal experience is one of the best ways of deepening your understanding of what you have read.

Share the following information about your adolescence with a partner.

1. Did you go through a growth spurt? At what age? Did it cause any problems?
2. Have you stopped growing? At what age did you stop?
3. Were you an early or a late bloomer? Do you think you had any advantages or disadvantages because of this? Explain.

The SQ3R System (Part 1) Ⓐ Ⓡ

SQ3R means Survey (*S*), Question (*Q*), Read, Recite, and Review (*3R*)

The SQ3R system is a five-step process that helps students become more active readers. Active readers do not simply pick up a text and read it. They perform a series of tasks before reading, while reading, and after reading; tasks that help them understand and remember what they have read.

In this prereading activity, we will look at the first three steps in the **SQ3R** system only: *survey*, *question*, and *read*.

A Step 1: *Survey* When you survey, or preview, a text before reading it closely, you look at titles, headings, subheadings, graphs, charts, pictures, and terms in bold or italics. You also skim, reading the beginning and end of some paragraphs.

Survey the text "Cognitive and Social Development in Adolescence." Then report back to the class about what you looked at and discovered.

B Step 2: *Question* Active readers formulate questions that they think the text will answer. As they read, they check to see if their questions are answered.

As a result of your survey of this text you can begin to formulate questions. How do you do this? One trick is to look at the headings, subheadings, and key terms that you noticed in your survey and turn them into questions. For example, the title of this text may suggest the following questions:

• What cognitive changes occur in adolescence?

• How does an adolescent develop socially? What changes take place?

Now survey this text again. In the margins, write questions that you expect the text to answer. When you go through the 3R steps (*read*, *recite*, and *review*), you will keep returning to these questions, asking yourself if you are able to answer them.

C Step 3: *Read* Imagine your instructor gave you an open-book test. As you were taking the test, you would look at the text to find the answers to the instructor's questions. When you read using the SQ3R system, you should read in the same way. You should be looking for the answers to the questions that you have asked yourself.

Reading 3

COGNITIVE AND SOCIAL DEVELOPMENT IN ADOLESCENCE

Adolescence is a developmental period in which, according to Piaget, one is now able to think abstractly and to imagine, to think about what is, and to ponder what might be. This new, higher level of mental operations often gets turned toward self-analysis, toward a contemplation of one's
5 self in a social context. In this section, we'll examine three issues related to cognitive and social processes in adolescent development: identity formation, adolescent egocentrism, and the influence of family.

Identity formation

Adolescents give the impression of being great experimenters. They experiment with hairstyles,
10 music, religions, drugs, sexual outlets, fad diets, part-time jobs, part-time relationships, and part-time philosophies of life. In fact, it often seems that teenagers' commitments are made on a part-time basis. They are busily trying things out, doing things
15 their way, off on a grand search for Truth.

Adolescence is a time for experimenting and searching for one's identity.

This perception of adolescents as experimenters is not without foundation. It is consistent with the view that one of the major tasks of adolescence is the resolution of an identity crisis – the struggle
20 to define and integrate the sense of who one is, what one is to do in life, and what one's attitudes, beliefs, and values should be. During adolescence, we come to grips with many questions: "Who am I?" "What am I going to do with my life?" "What
25 is the point of it all?" Needless to say, these are not trivial questions. A person's search for his or her identity may lead to conflicts. Some of these conflicts may be resolved very easily, some continue into adulthood.

The concept of identity formation is associated with the personality
30 theorist Erik Erikson. For Erikson, the search for identity is the fifth of eight stages of psychosocial development. This stage occurs during the adolescent years. For some youngsters, adolescence brings very little confusion or conflict at all in terms of attitudes, beliefs, or values. Many teenagers are quite able and willing to accept without question
35 the values and sense of self that they began to develop in childhood.

For many teenagers, however, the conflict of identity is quite real. They have a sense of giving up the values of parents and teachers in favor of new ones – their own. On the other hand, physical growth, physiological changes, increased sexuality, and perceived societal
40 pressures to decide what they want to be when they "grow up" may lead

to what Erikson calls "role confusion." Wanting to be independent, to be one's self, often does not fit in with the values of the past, of childhood. Hence, the teenager tries to experiment with different possibilities in an attempt to see what works out best, occasionally to 45 the dissatisfaction of bewildered parents.

Figure 3.2 Stages 5–8 of Erikson's Stages of Psychosocial Development

Stage	Issue to Resolve	Description of Stage
5. Adolescence	Identity vs. role confusion	Teenagers test out different identities until they form a single identity. If they are unable to, they may remain confused about who they are.
6. Early adulthood	Intimacy vs. isolation	Young adults struggle to form close relationships and gain ability for an intimate loving relationship. If they don't, they may feel socially isolated.
7. Middle adulthood	Generativity vs. stagnation	At this age, people try to contribute to the world, usually through family or work. If they don't achieve this, they may feel a lack of purpose.
8. Late adulthood	Integrity vs. despair	When looking back at his or her life, the older adult feels a sense of satisfaction. If this does not happen, he or she may feel a sense of despair.

Erik Erikson

Adolescent egocentrism

Egocentrism – a focusing on one's self and an inability to take the point of view of others – was used by Piaget to describe part of the cognitive functioning of young children (between the 50 ages of two and six). David Elkind uses the term "egocentrism" in a slightly different way. In adolescent egocentrism, not only do individuals engage in self-centered thinking, but they also come to believe that virtually everyone else is 55 thinking about them, too. Because they can now think abstractly, adolescents begin to think about the thoughts of others and have a tendency to believe that they are usually the focus of attention. Needless to say, adolescent 60 egocentrism often leads to a heightened sense of self-consciousness.

Elkind proposes two particular manifestations of adolescent egocentrism. For one thing, teenagers often feel that they are constantly "on stage," performing. They become quite convinced that when they
65 enter a room, everyone is watching them and making judgments about everything – from what they are wearing to how their hair is styled. Now, in truth, it may be that no one is watching, but the youngster believes that they are. Elkind calls this the construction of an **imaginary audience**. Coming to think that everyone is watching
70 and analyzing you is explanation enough for the extreme self-consciousness of many young teens, argues Elkind.

Adolescents often tend to overemphasize their own importance. They are, after all, the focus of their own attention, and given their imaginary audiences, they feel they are the focus of everyone else's
75 attention as well. As a result, they tend to develop some rather unrealistic cognitions about themselves, which Elkind calls "personal fables." These are essentially stories about themselves that teenagers generate, often on the basis of irrational beliefs. They come to believe (egocentrically) that no harm can come to them. They won't become
80 addicted after trying a drug at a party. Their driving won't be affected by alcohol consumption. They won't get pregnant. Those sorts of things happen to others. These sorts of beliefs (cognitions) can be dangerous, of course, and they can be the source of considerable parental aggravation.

The influence of family

85 No matter what label we give it, one of the major processes involved in adolescence is separating in some real way from one's family. With the emergence of one's own identity comes independence and autonomy. The resulting conflict for teenagers is often very real. On the one hand, they want to become autonomous and strike out on their own. At
90 the same time, they sense sadness and even fear over giving up the security of home and family.

How adolescents resolve conflicts they have with their parents often hinges significantly on what is termed *parental style*. Psychologists have identified three major approaches used by parents in dealing
95 with their adolescent children. (It should be pointed out quickly that few parents adopt and use one and only one style). The *authoritarian* style of parenting decrees that, "You should do so, because I say so!" As often as not, the adolescent isn't even allowed to express his or her beliefs. The teenager is seen as a member of low standing in family
100 affairs. Not surprisingly, this style of parenting behavior often leads to rebellion, alienation, and more conflict. On the other hand, the authoritarian style can lead to submissiveness and conformity, which, for the emerging teenager, is maladaptive. The style of parenting called *permissive* is in many ways at the
105 other extreme from the authoritarian style. Here, the teenager has an almost free rein. Parents are supportive but set few limits. The style most recommended is usually called *democratic*. Here, parents act as experts,
110 give advice, and do set limits, but they also consult with the teenager, allow some independence of choice, and involve the teenager in decision making.

Most teenagers feel that their parents use
115 a democratic style and they value that style. Reports of family difficulties with adolescents can often be traced to either an overly authoritarian or overly permissive style.

Most teenagers prefer a democratic style of parenting.

Teenage Suicide

Tragically, around the world, suicide is one of the leading causes of death among teenagers aged 15 to 19. It is the second leading cause of death for females (after traffic accidents) and the third leading cause for males (after accidents and assault). According to the World Health Organization (WHO), approximately 7.5 children in every 100,000 commit suicide, with the rate being much higher for males (10.5) than females (4.1).

One of the most disturbing phenomena is that sometimes suicides suddenly occur in clusters; that is, one child kills himself or herself, then another child does the same in a nearby house or town, and then another. Even more disturbing is a recent phenomenon in some countries where groups of young people commit suicide together.

Even with the high rate of teenage suicide, the WHO estimates that their data may not be that reliable because, for cultural and religious reasons, suicides are often underreported.

Fig. 3.3 Selected suicide rates per 100,000 around the world. Data is given for countries reporting after 2000.

	Male	Female
Russia	39	9
Belarus	24	4
Canada	16	5
Australia	14	4
U.S.A.	13	3
Japan	9	4
South Korea	6	5
Germany	9	3
Sweden	6	3

Source: WHO

1 Taking notes in the margins Ⓐ Ⓦ

Taking notes while you read can be an effective study tool. Some students like to write notes in the margins of their textbooks. These are called "marginal notes." Others prefer to use a separate notebook.

A Work with a partner and discuss the following questions.

1. What are the advantages of marginal notes over notes in a notebook?

2. What are the disadvantages of marginal notes compared to notes in a notebook?

3. Which do you prefer? Why?

B Look at the sample marginal notes taken on a portion of this text, shown in Figure A on page 79. Answer these questions with a partner.

1. What abbreviations does the note-taker use?

2. What kind of information does the note-taker put in the margins of the text?

3. How does the note-taker identify key terms, their definitions, and important names?

4. How does the note-taker draw attention to examples or details in the text?

C Look at the portion of the text under the heading "Adolescent Egocentrism" on page 71 and make marginal notes as directed in the following steps.

1. Highlight the following key terms and their definitions.
  • egocentrism
  • imaginary audience
  • adolescent egocentrism
  • personal fables

2. Draw vertical lines and put the following notes next to them, opposite the parts of the text to which they refer.
  • What is Adol. Egocent?
  • Piaget def. of Egocent (2–6 yr olds)
  • Elkind def. of Adol. Egocent.
  • Ex. of adol. self-consciousness
  • Exs. of dangerous unrealistic beliefs

3. Underline and put an asterisk (*) next to the phrase "two particular manifestations of adolescent egocentrism" and then draw two lines from the word *two*: one line to the term *imaginary audience* and the other to *personal fables.*

4. Write the numbers *1*, *2*, and *3* in the text over the three examples of dangerous beliefs teenagers have.

D Make your own marginal notes for the third section of this reading, The Influence of Family. Compare your marginal notes with a partner's.

2 The SQ3R System (Part 2) Ⓐ Ⓡ

> The SQ3R system includes not only prereading strategies, but also strategies to use after reading a text – Steps 4 and 5, below.

A Step 4: *Recite* The fourth step in the SQ3R system is to recite. To recite is to say aloud from memory. After you read a section of text, you should stop and repeat it in your own words. Ask yourself, "Now what did I just read? Do I understand the main ideas? Can I answer the questions that I thought this text would answer for me?"

Choose one of the three parts of the text "Cognitive and Social Development in Adolescence." Reread it. Then give an oral summary to a student who read a different part of the text.

B Step 5: *Review* When you review a section or chapter of a textbook, you should go back and skim the text, placing a check (✓) next to the parts of the text that you are sure you understand and a question mark (?) next to those parts that are still unclear to you and that you need to study further.

Review the whole text, "Cognitive and Social Development in Adolescence," placing checks and question marks where appropriate.

3 Synonyms Ⓥ Ⓡ

> Writers often don't like to repeat the same word or phrase in their writing. Instead, they use synonyms, or words and phrases that are similar in meaning. Knowing this can sometimes help you when you come across an unfamiliar word or phrase. You can look forward or backward in the text for a word or phrase that might have the same meaning or a similar meaning.

Read the following excerpts from the text and find a synonym, either before or after the word or phrase in bold. Circle the synonymous word or phrase on the line as in the example.

1. Adolescence is a developmental period in which, according to Piaget, one is now able to think abstractly and to imagine, to (think about) what is, and to **ponder** what might be.

2. This new, higher level of mental operations often gets turned toward self-analysis, toward a **contemplation of one's self** in a social context.

3. Adolescents give the impression of being great experimenters. They experiment with hairstyles, music. . . . They are busily **trying things out**, doing things their way, off on a grand search for Truth.

4. . . . one of the major tasks of adolescence is the resolution of an identity crisis – the struggle to define and integrate the sense of who one is, what one is to do in life. . . . During adolescence, we **come to grips with** many questions: "Who am I?" "What am I going to do with my life?"

5. Elkind proposes two particular manifestations of adolescent egocentrism. For one thing, teenagers often feel that they are constantly "on stage," **performing**.

6. As a result, they tend to develop some rather **unrealistic cognitions** about themselves, which Elkind calls *personal fables.* These are essentially stories about themselves that teenagers generate, often on the basis of irrational beliefs.

7. With the emergence of one's own identity comes independence and **autonomy**. The resulting conflict for teenagers is often very real.

8. The style most recommended is usually called *democratic.* Here, parents act as experts, give advice, and do set limits, but they also **consult with the teenager**, allow some independence of choice, and involve the teenager in decision making.

4 Thinking critically ®

Often a writer includes a short, separate text in a box, but does not refer to it anywhere. It is then your responsibility to read the text and think about how the topic of the boxed text is related to the topic of the reading.

A Read the boxed text "Teenage Suicide." Think about how this text relates to some of the information in any of the three readings in this chapter.

B Work with a partner and discuss how you think the topic relates to the chapter topic.

C Also discuss some of the statistics and whether they are surprising to you.

5 Personalizing the topic ®

Answer the following questions with your classmates. Explain each answer fully.

1. During your adolescence, were you a "great experimenter"?
2. During your adolescence, did you go through an identity crisis?
3. Can you relate to the concepts of an imaginary audience and personal fables? Were they a part of your adolescence?
4. What style of parenting did your parents adopt? Do you approve of this style? What style of parenting do you believe is best?

Chapter 3 Academic Vocabulary Review

The following are some of the words that appear in Chapter 3. They all come from the Academic Word List, a list of words that researchers have discovered occur frequently in many different types of academic texts. If you can learn these words, it should help you when you have a reading in almost any academic discipline. For a complete list of all the Academic Word List words in this chapter and in all the other readings in this book, see the Appendix on pages 213–214.

Reading 1 Defining Adolescence	Reading 2 Physical Change in Adolescence	Reading 3 Cognitive and Social Development in Adolescence
approximately conflict (n) perspective specify survive transition (n)	evidence impact (v) resolve (v) status theorist undergo whereas	constantly foundation hence integrate period

Complete the following sentences with words from the lists above.

1. Which _____ of life involves the greatest amount of change?

2. It is not unusual for there to be _____ in very large families.

3. Parents should _____ be watching their children for signs of depression.

4. I understand your viewpoint, but I have a different _____ on the subject.

5. At what age do people in your country legally achieve adult _____?

6. Which _____ says that it is healthy for children to rebel against their parents?

7. _____ 50 percent of the population of India is under the age of 25.

8. When two people disagree, they should try to _____ the issue peacefully, not violently.

9. Some people _____ a tremendous number of physical changes during their teen years.

10. The _____ from adolescence to adulthood is not always easy.

11. Young adolescents are often very self-conscious; _____ they tend to avoid having to talk in public.

12. There is no _____ that the girl committed suicide.

IDENTITY FORMATION

What is identity formation?

Adolescents give the impression of being great experimenters. They experiment with hair styles, music, religions, drugs, sexual outlets, fad diets, part-time jobs, part-time relationships, and part-time philosophies of life. In fact, it often seems that teenagers' commitments are made on a part-time basis. They are busily trying out, doing things their way, off on a grand search for Truth.

Things adols. like to experiment w/

This perception of adolescents as experimenters is not without foundation. It is consistent with the view that one of the major tasks of adolescence is the resolution of an *identity crisis* – the struggle to define and integrate the sense of who one is, what one is to do in life, and what one's attitudes, beliefs, and values should be. During adolescence, we come to grips with many questions: "Who am I?" "What am I going to do with my life?" "What is the point of it all?" Needless to say, these are not trivial questions. A person's search for his or her identity may lead to conflicts. Some of these conflicts may be resolved very easily, some continue into adulthood.

Def. of identity crisis

The big questions adols. ask

The concept of *identity formation* is associated with the personality theorist* <u>Erik Erikson</u>. For Erikson, the search for identity is the fifth of eight stages of psychosocial development. It is the stage that occurs during the adolescent years. For some youngsters, adolescence brings very little confusion or conflict at all in terms of attitudes, beliefs, or values. Many teenagers are quite able and willing to accept without question the values and sense of self that they began to develop in childhood.

Not all adols. question values

For many teenagers, however, the conflict of identity is quite real. They have a sense of giving up the values of parents and teachers in favor of new ones – their own. On the other hand, physical growth, physiological changes, and increased sexuality, and perceived societal pressures to decide that they want to be when they "grow up" may lead to what Erikson calls *role confusion*. Wanting to be independent, to be one's self, often does not fit in with the values of the past, of childhood. Hence, the teenager tries to experiment with different possibilities in an attempt to see what works out best, occasionally to the dissatisfaction of bewildered parents.

Conflict = own values vs parents

Causes of role confusion

Figure A Sample marginal notes on "Cognitive and Social Development in Adolescence"

Developing Writing Skills

In this section, you will learn about paraphrasing: what it is and how to do it. At the end of the unit, you will be given your essay assignment in which you will be asked to use information from the readings in the unit. When you include this information in your essay, you will use your paraphrasing skills.

Paraphrasing

Sometimes when you have a writing assignment, you read something that someone else wrote that has information and ideas that you want to include in your writing, too. You cannot simply copy this person's words into your writing and pretend that they are your own. This is called *plagiarism*, and it is considered to be a serious offense. However, you can paraphrase. Paraphrasing involves understanding the meaning of what someone else wrote and then *using your own language* to express the same thing.

Paraphrasing is an important and valuable skill, but it takes a lot of practice to do it well. The key to writing a good paraphrase is not only to use synonyms, but also to change the sentence structure.

Here are some steps that can help you write a successful paraphrase.
1. Read what you want to paraphrase many times.
2. Make certain that you completely understand the meaning.
3. Make brief notes to help you remember the meaning, but use different words from the original in your notes.
4. Put aside the original and wait a few minutes.
5. Write your paraphrase without looking back at the original.
6. Compare your paraphrase to the original. Make sure that you have used different words (synonyms) and phrases from the original and different sentence structure, too.

A Work with a partner. Compare this sentence from the article "Defining Adolescence" with its paraphrase. Make a list of all the synonyms that the writer used.

Some psychologists consider this a period of growth and positive change; others view adolescence as a period of great turmoil, stress, rebellion, and negativism.

Some psychologists perceive this as a time of positive change and development, others see adolescence as a time of tremendous difficulty, rebelliousness, negativity, and stress.

B Look at this paraphrase of the same sentence. Make a list of all the changes that the writer made.

> Psychologists differ in how they perceive adolescence. For some, it is a dark period, full of problems and stress. Others, however, think of this period positively, for giving adolescents a chance to grow and develop.

C Compare the three paraphrases below this sentence from "Physical Change in Adolescence." Discuss which you think is the most acceptable paraphrase, and why.

Some late-maturing girls . . . feel – at least in retrospect – that being a late bloomer was an advantage because it offered them an opportunity to develop some broad interests, rather than becoming "boy crazy" like so many of their peers in early adolescence.

a) When they look back at their adolescence, it is not unusual for some girls who matured later than their peers to feel that being a late bloomer was a positive thing. They were able to develop a wide range of new interests instead of always thinking about boys, like so many of their friends.

b) Some late-maturing girls think in retrospect that they had an advantage because they matured later than their peers. While their early maturing peers were often boy crazy, they had the opportunity to develop broad interests during their adolescence.

c) Unlike their early maturing friends who always seemed to be thinking about boys, some late-maturing girls believe that being a late bloomer gave them an advantage. It gave them the opportunity to explore a broad range of interests.

D Write a paraphrase of each of the following pieces of text from "Cognitive and Social Development in Adolescence." Follow the guidelines on page 80.

a) Wanting to be independent, to be one's self, often does not fit in with the values of the past, of childhood. Hence, the teenager tries to experiment with different possibilities in an attempt to see what works out best, occasionally to the dissatisfaction of bewildered parents.

b) With the emergence of one's own identity comes independence and autonomy. The resulting conflict for teenagers is often very real. On the one hand, they want to become autonomous and strike out on their own. At the same time, they sense sadness and even fear over giving up the security of home and family.

E Compare your paraphrases with a partner's. Notice the differences. Choose one of your paraphrases and work together to improve it.

Chapter 4
Adulthood

1 Personalizing the topic Ⓡ

A According to this text, young adults have to face many difficult questions. Which of these questions, taken from the text, have you ever seriously asked yourself? Put a check [✓] in front of those that apply.

___ **1.** Should I get married?

___ **2.** Should I live with someone?

___ **3.** Should I get a job?

___ **4.** To what sort of career should I devote my life?

___ **5.** Do I need more education?

___ **6.** Where should I go to get more education?

___ **7.** Should I have children?

___ **8.** When should I have children?

B Compare your answers with a partner's. Discuss which were the most difficult questions to deal with, and why.

2 Previewing art and graphics Ⓡ

> By previewing any graphs, diagrams, charts, photographs, or illustrations, you can stimulate your critical thinking skills before you start reading.

A Look at the graphs on pages 84 and 86 and then answer the following questions with a partner.

1. What do the graphs show?

2. Do any of these data surprise you? Why or why not?

3. How do you explain the data in Figure 4.1? Think of at least three different reasons that might explain trends that are clearly seen in these graphs.

4. How do you explain the data in Figures 4.2 and 4.3? Think of at least three different reasons that might explain the trends that are clearly seen in these graphs.

B Share your answers with the class.

Reading 1

EARLY ADULTHOOD

Just when adulthood begins is difficult to say. In a legal sense, adult status is often granted by governments – at age 18 for some activities or at age 21 for others. Psychologically speaking, adulthood is marked by two possibilities that at first seem contradictory: (1) independence,
5 in the sense of taking responsibility for one's actions and no longer being tied to parents and (2) interdependence, in the sense of building new commitments and intimacies in interpersonal relationships.

In the past, there was little argument that adulthood abruptly followed the end of adolescence. However, some developmental
10 psychologists have begun to argue recently that there is an in-between period when the individual is no longer an adolescent, but has also not yet taken on full adulthood status and independence. This period has been called **emerging adulthood**, a term coined in 2000 by developmental psychologist J. J. Arnett in a much cited article
15 in *Psychology Today*. According to Arnett, young people from their late teens to their late twenties are increasingly going through an experimental period of self-exploration. They are delaying marriage and experimenting with work and love. They are also likely to still be somewhat dependent on their parents, who may continue to give
20 them both some financial and emotional support.

emerging adulthood
a term used by some to describe a time when one is no longer an adolescent and not yet fully an adult

Arnett describes the psychological outlook of young people in their late teens to late twenties as being very different from the outlook of young people of the same age 50 years earlier. Young people of that era, Arnett says, were "eager to enter adulthood and settle down."
25 However, his claim is that the emerging adults of the twenty-first century have a very different attitude.... marriage, home, and children are seen by most of them not as achievements to be pursued, but as perils to be avoided. It is not that most of them do not want marriage, a home, and (one or two) children – eventually. Most of them do want
30 to take on all these adult obligations, and most of them will have done so by the time they reach the age of 30. It is just that, in their late teens and early twenties, they ponder these obligations and think, "Yes, but not yet." Adulthood and its obligations offer security and stability, but they also represent a closing of doors – the end of independence, the
35 end of spontaneity, the end of a sense of wide-open possibilities.

Fig. 4.1 Median age of men and women at first marriage in U.S., 1970–2008

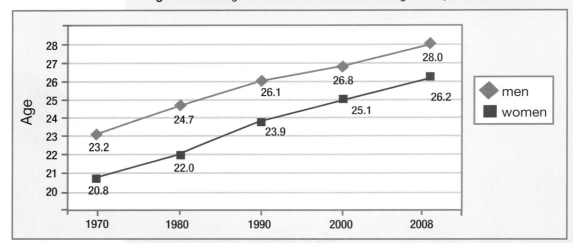

Source: U.S. Census Bureau, Current Population Survey, 2005; American Community Survey

We have seen how developmental psychologist Erik Erikson regards adolescence as the period when individuals struggle with identity formation. However, Arnett thinks that this period now extends well into an individual's twenties and is in fact more marked
40 during that period. Hence, like adolescence, emerging adulthood is a period of some anxiety and uncertainty. It is during this period, as the emerging adult moves towards attaining adult status, that there are new and often difficult choices to be made. Should I get married? Should I stay single? Perhaps I should live with someone. Should I get
45 a job? Which one? To what sort of career should I devote my life? Do I need more education? What sort of education? Where? How? Should I have children? How many? When? Now, while I'm young, or should I wait until I'm more experienced and have an established career?

Work

One of the most pressing decisions at this time of one's life is what
50 career to pursue. However, with so many possibilities from which
to choose, this decision is often a difficult one to make. In addition,
there are many factors that may influence an individual in the choice
of a career and some of these may be conflicting. For example, family
pressure, the potential for earning money, and one's own personal
55 interests may all be factors that pull an individual in three different
directions when trying to decide what career path to follow. Although
it is often assumed that by the time a person is a young adult they
will know what they want to "do with their life," in fact the process
of finding a career may take a long time. It is not uncommon for an
60 individual to try more than one career before finding the one that leads
to job satisfaction.

Marriage

The other pressing decision during these years revolves
around what Erikson describes as the basic choice
of intimacy versus isolation (see chart on page
65 71). Failure to establish close, loving, or intimate
relationships, according to Erikson, results in
loneliness and long periods of social isolation.
More typically, however, this conflict results in
a loving monogamous relationship, ending in
70 marriage. Marriage is certainly not the only
source of interpersonal intimacy, but it is still
the first choice for most Americans. While more
young adults than ever before are postponing
marriage plans, fully 95 percent of Americans
75 do marry (at least once).

Parenthood

Becoming a parent is generally taken as a sure
sign of adulthood. Yet here again young people all
around the world are putting off having their first baby
until much later than earlier generations (see Figure 4.3).
80 In several developed countries, the average age for a woman to have
her first child is now almost 30 (see Figure 4.3). Once there is a baby
around the house, established routines become significantly changed,
often leading to negative consequences. The freedom for spontaneous
trips, intimate outings, and privacy is in large measure given up in
85 trade for the joys of parenthood. As parents, men and women take
on new responsibilities – those of father and mother. These new roles
of adulthood add to the already established roles of being a male or a
female, a son or a daughter, a husband or a wife.

Fig. 4.2 Average age of mother at first birth in U.S., 1970–2006

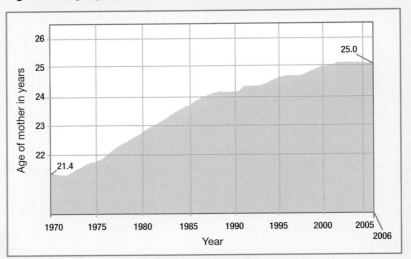

Source: CDC/NCHS, National Vital Statistics System

Fig. 4.3 Mean age of women at birth of first child in various countries, 2008

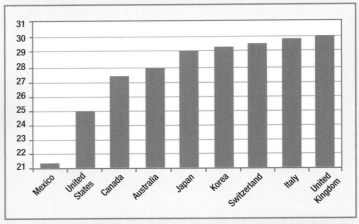

Source: OECD Family Database www.oedc.org/els/social/family/database
OECD–/social Pollicy Division–Directorate of Employment, Labour and Social Affairs

Clearly young adulthood is a period of stress. It is a time for
90 raising a family, finding and maintaining the "right" job, and keeping
a balance among self, family, job, and society at large. It is a period
of life that requires great energy. Fortunately, in terms of physical
development, we are at something of a peak during our 20s and 30s.
As Levinson (1986) has stated, "early adulthood is the era of greatest
95 energy and abundance and of greatest contradiction and stress."

1 Reading actively ®

Sometimes a writer does not provide examples to the reader. When that happens, it is important for you to be an active reader and to think of examples that the writer could have included. This will deepen your understanding of the reading. It can also help you later if you are tested on a reading or have to write about the reading. You will be able to show your own original thinking.

Read excerpts from the reading and answer the questions that follow them with a partner.

1. "In a legal sense, adult status is often granted by governments – at age 18 for some activities or at age 21 for others." What activities? Think of examples the writer could have used.

2. "Psychologically speaking, adulthood is marked by two possibilities . . . (1) independence . . . and (2) interdependence, in the sense of building new commitments and intimacies in interpersonal relationships." What new relationships? Think of examples the writer could have used.

3. ". . . young people . . . are increasingly going through an experimental period. . . . They are . . . experimenting with work and love." What examples might the writer have given here?

4. "Once there is a baby around the house, established routines become significantly changed, often leading to negative consequences." What routines? What negative consequences?

5. "The freedom for . . . trips . . . outings . . . privacy is in large measure given up in trade for the joys of parenthood." What are these joys?

6. "Fortunately, in terms of physical development, we are at something of a peak during our 20s and 30s." What examples could the writer have given here?

2 Collocations Ⓥ Ⓦ

When learning vocabulary in English, it is always a good idea to be aware of *collocations*, or combinations of words that often occur together. Some verbs, for example, are often followed by – or *collocate with* – certain nouns. The more collocations you know, the easier reading becomes.

A Make verb + noun collocations by writing the verbs on the line in front of the nouns they collocate with in the reading. Be careful, because sometimes the noun may be separated from the verb by several other words, and sometimes the verb may even come after the noun.

1. to go through (Line 16)   _____ a path

2. to give (Line 19)   _____ money

3. to make (Line 43)   _____ a career

4. to pursue (Line 50)   _____ relationships

5. to choose from (Line 51)   _____ responsibilities

6. to earn (Line 54)   _____ support

7. to follow (Line 56)   _____ a period

8. to establish (Line 65)   _____ a family

9. to take on (Line 85)   _____ choices

10. to raise (Line 90)   _____ possibilities

B Compare your answers with a partner's.

C What other verb + noun collocations could you make from this list? Share your ideas with the class.

3 Using data from a graphic Ⓦ Ⓡ

A lot of data are often contained in a graph or a chart that accompanies a text. Usually only some of that information is referred to in the reading. It is up to you to examine the chart or graph in detail. You should then try writing about the graph in your own words. This may help you when you have to write about the data in an essay or remember the data for a test.

A Read the following description of Figure 4.1 on page 84 and answer the questions that follow.

Figure 4.1 shows the median age at which men and women in the United States first got married between 1970 and 2008. As can be seen, every year between 1970 and 2008 the median age of first marriage for both men and women went up. For example, for men, it went up by 4.8 years, from 23.2 in 1970 to 28.0 in 2008. For women, it went up by 5.4 years. In 1970, the median age at first marriage for women was just over 20 years of age, but by 2008 the median age was 26.2 years. One possible explanation for these data is that following the women's liberation movement, which took hold in the 1960s and flourished in the 1970s, women were looking to get more education, get better jobs, and become more independent.

1. In what order did the writer organize this description of the graph? Put the following elements in order from 1 to 4.

  ____ **a.** Some specific data that support the main finding

  ____ **b.** An attempt to understand why the data show what they do

  ____ **c.** A neutral description stating what the graph contains

  ____ **d.** A description of the main finding of the graph

2. Draw lines in the paragraph above to show where each element begins and ends.

3. Circle the language that the writer used to introduce each element.

B Work with a partner and write a description of either Figure 4.2 or Figure 4.3 on page 86. Use the same order of elements that the writer used above and the same language to introduce each element.

4 Journal writing

Many language learners keep a private journal and write about personal events and ideas. It is a good way to practice writing in a second language without worrying too much about accuracy or a grade. When you read about a topic that interests you, even in an academic textbook, take some time to write down your personal thoughts on the topic.

Write a journal entry on one or more of the following topics from the reading:

Work

1. Why I chose my career
2. The career that I wish I had
3. Why I can't decide what career I want

Marriage

1. Why I never want to get married
2. Why I want to get married
3. Why I got married

Parenthood

1. Why I never want to have children
2. The age at which I want to have children
3. Why I had children

1 Thinking about the topic ®

A At about the age of 40, a number of physical changes begin to take place in people. Make a list of five to eight such changes. Here are some sentence starters to give you ideas:

The hair begins to . . .

The muscles begin to . . .

The stomach begins to . . .

The skin begins to . . .

B Compare your list with a partner's.

2 Guessing meaning from context Ⓥ Ⓡ

You do not need to look up every word that you do not know in the dictionary. It is often possible to get a general idea of the meaning of a word or phrase from its context. In addition, the form of a word can sometimes give you a clue to its meaning. If you look at its parts, it may remind you of other words that you know that belong in the same word family.

Read the following passage from the text and use the context and the form of the words to work out what the words in bold probably mean.

Middle adulthood is also a period that involves **transition** and reexamination. During the middle years, one is forced to **contemplate** one's own **mortality**. The so-called **middle-age spread,** loss of muscle tone, **facial wrinkles**, and **graying** hair are evident each day in the mirror. At about the age of 40, **sensory capacities** and abilities begin to **diminish** slowly.

1. transition _____

2. contemplate _____

3. mortality _____

4. middle-age spread _____

5. facial wrinkles _____

6. graying _____

7. sensory capacities _____

8. diminish _____

Reading 2

MIDDLE ADULTHOOD

It is more difficult to generalize about adulthood stages than about life's early years. If you know that Jamie is a one-year-old and Jamal is a 10-year-old, you could say a great deal about each child. Not so with adults who differ by the same number of years. The boss may be
5 30 or 60; the marathon runner may be 20 or 50; a 19-year-old can be a parent who supports a child or a child who gets financial help from his or her parents. Yet our life courses are in some ways similar. Physically, cognitively, and especially socially, we are at age 50 different from our 25-year-old selves.

10   As the middle years of adulthood approach, many aspects of life become settled. By the time most people reach the age of 40, their place in the framework of society is fairly well set. They have chosen their lifestyle and have grown accustomed to it. They have a family (or have decided not to). They have chosen what is to be their major life
15 work or career.

Returning to Erik Erikson one more time, Erikson claims that this period of life for many people is dominated in some way by the concept of **generativity** (see chart on page 71). This means that during middle adulthood, our focus tends to shift from a focus on ourselves
20 to a focus on future generations. For those who have children, that focus is clearly expressed by the efforts to bring up a new generation. Even for those who don't have children, generativity can be expressed by feeling the need to contribute to society and create a better future for those who will follow you.

generativity
Erikson's term for working for the good of the next generation

25   Middle adulthood is also a period that involves transition and reexamination. During the middle years, one is forced to contemplate one's own mortality. The so-called "middle-age spread," loss of muscle tone, facial wrinkles, and graying hair are evident each day in the mirror. At about the age of 40, sensory capacities and abilities begin to
30 diminish slowly.

    As people progress through middle age, they realize that most of their life is behind them. For some, this produces something of a crisis – what is commonly called a "midlife crisis." The popular image of the midlife crisis for a man is someone who gives up his family
35 for a younger girlfriend and a hot sports car. The popular image of a woman having a midlife crisis is someone who starts to dress like her teenage daughter, dyes her hair, and has cosmetic surgery.

    Is the midlife crisis a reality or a stereotype? Surveys of large samples of people reveal in fact that unhappiness, job dissatisfaction,
40 marital dissatisfaction, divorce, and suicide do not surge during the early 40s. Divorce, for example, is more common among those in their 20s, suicide among those in their 70s and 80s. One study of emotional stability in nearly 10,000 men and women found "not the slightest evidence" that distress peaks anywhere in the midlife range.
45 Additionally, for the one in four adults who do report experiencing a midlife crisis, the trigger is not age, but a major life event such as illness, divorce, or job loss.

    Even when children leave home, while this can be a difficult separation for the parents, it does not generally lead to a time of crisis.
50 National surveys have revealed that the "empty nest," as it is called, is for most people a happy place. Research has shown that, compared with middle-aged women with children at home, those living in an empty nest report greater happiness and greater enjoyment of their marriage. For many parents, it has even been described as a "second
55 honeymoon."

The Seven Challenges of Middle Adulthood

Richard Havighurst has identified seven major tasks that one has to face during one's middle years.

    1. Accepting and adjusting to physiological changes

    2. Reaching and maintaining satisfactory performance in one's job

    3. Adjusting to having aging parents

    4. Assisting teenage children to become happy and responsible adults

    5. Achieving social and civic responsibility

    6. Relating to one's spouse

    7. Developing new adult leisure-time activities

1 Paragraph topics Ⓦ Ⓡ

> When you read, you should try to identify the topic of each paragraph – what the paragraph is about. When you write, each paragraph should also have one clear topic.

Match the following topics to their paragraphs. Write the number of the paragraph next to the topic.

____ A definition of *generativity*

____ Description of midlife crises in men and women

____ An evaluation of whether midlife crises are normal

____ The typical middle-aged adult

____ What happens when children leave home

____ Physical changes in middle adulthood

____ Differences between people at different ages

2 Paragraph main ideas Ⓦ Ⓡ

> The topic of a paragraph is what the paragraph is about. The main idea is what the writer wants to say about the topic. Identifying a topic's main idea is one of the most important reading skills. When you write, you should also have a clear idea of what your paragraph topics are and what you are trying to say about each topic – your main ideas.

A Match the following five main ideas to their paragraphs. Notice how the main idea says something about the topic. Write the number of the paragraph next to the main idea.

____ The midlife crisis is more of a stereotype than a reality.

____ When children leave home, middle-aged parents don't usually have a crisis.

____ *Generativity* is defined as focusing one's efforts on the needs of younger people.

____ It is not easy to make generalizations about the different stages of adulthood.

____ A typical middle-aged adult has usually made most of life's major decisions.

B Find the topics of the other two paragraphs, look back at those paragraphs in the text, and write sentences that capture the main idea of each one.

C Compare your answers with a partner's.

3 Supporting main ideas Ⓦ Ⓡ

> A well-written paragraph should have both a main idea and support for that main idea. Analyzing paragraphs in your reading to see how a main idea is supported will help you create well-structured paragraphs when you write.

A Reread Paragraph 6. Find the main idea from Task 2 and write it on the line below. Then answer the questions that follow.

_____

1. How does the information about divorce support the main idea?
2. How does the information about suicide support the main idea?
3. How does the study of emotional stability support the main idea?
4. How does the statistic about the 25 percent of adults who experience a midlife crisis support the main idea?

B Complete the outline of Paragraph 6 in note form.

Main Idea: _____

    Support 1: Divorce more common _____

    Support 2: _____ common in _____

    Support 3: Emotional stability study = distress _____

    Support 4: If crisis, not from age but _____

C Create an outline of Paragraph 7.

4 Applying what you have read Ⓡ Ⓦ

> Try to apply the information that you have just learned about in your reading. If you can do this, you will be able to achieve a deeper understanding of the ideas and information in a reading.

A Look again at the list of seven major challenges that people usually have to face during middle adulthood in the boxed text on page 92.

Think about a middle-aged person whom you know well (perhaps one of your parents). Write the relationship of this person to you on the line, for example, _aunt_ or _friend_. Then put a check (✓) next to the challenges that this person has faced.

My _____ has had to face these challenges:

1. adjusting to physiological changes of middle age ☐
2. struggling with one's career ☐
3. taking care of aging parents ☐
4. trying to help teenage children become responsible adults ☐
5. finding ways to play a role in the community ☐
6. developing a stronger relationship with one's spouse ☐
7. finding new hobbies or leisure interests ☐

B Describe this person to a partner or to the class. Talk about the challenges he or she has met.

5 Synthesizing Ⓐ Ⓡ

> After you read two selections that are on the same or a similar topic, one way to prepare for a test is to make a chart that shows points of similarity or difference.

A Reread "Early Adulthood" on pages 83–86. Then complete the chart below with notes to show contrasts between early and middle adulthood.

	Early Adulthood	**Middle Adulthood**
Physically	*at a peak*	
Relationships		*settled as either single or married*
Jobs		*established and usually satisfied*
Personal focus	*on self*	
Children	*may have very young children*	
New responsibilities		*for aging parents*

B Compare your chart with a partner's. Add any details that you may have missed.

1 Thinking about the topic ®

A In this text, you will read about the elderly. Before you read, respond to the following statements about the elderly people in a country that you know well. If you agree strongly, circle *1*. If you disagree strongly, circle *4*.

	Strongly agree			*Strongly disagree*
Most elderly people . . .				
a. feel negative about their lives	1	2	3	4
b. are lonely	1	2	3	4
c. have serious health problems	1	2	3	4
d. live inactive lives	1	2	3	4
e. have many financial worries	1	2	3	4
f. fear death and dying	1	2	3	4

B Compare your answers with a partner's.

2 Examining graphics ®

It is always a good habit to examine the graphics in a text before you start reading. It is also a good study skill to write about the graphs and charts in a text. Remember that a typical way to write about a chart is to write about the following elements in the order given.

- What data was used to create the chart
- The main finding of the chart
- A specific detail or two from the chart
- A possible explanation for the data in the chart

A Work with a partner and plan a description of Figures 4.4 and 4.5.

B Choose either Figure 4.4 or Figure 4.5 and write a description.

3 Increasing reading speed ®

Use this text as an opportunity to practice your speed-reading skills. Before you start, review the guidelines for faster reading on page 35 in Chapter 2.

Read the text "Late Adulthood" to practice reading for speed. (Do not read the boxed text "Do You Want to Live to Be 100?") Time yourself. When you finish, turn to the tasks that begin on page 100 and write down how long it took you to read the text.

Reading 3

LATE ADULTHOOD

The elderly are now the fastest growing segment of the population. Increasing life expectancy (humanity's greatest achievement, some would say) combined with decreasing birthrates make the elderly a larger and larger proportion of the population. This fact gives rise to
5 several questions: Is it desirable to live longer? What quality of life can we expect when we enter our period of late adulthood? Do positive or negative experiences await us?

Overall outlook on life

From early adulthood to middle adulthood, people typically experience
10 a strengthening sense of identity, confidence, and self-esteem. In later life, challenges arise. Income shrinks, work is often taken away, the body deteriorates, recall fades, energy
15 wanes, family members and friends die or move away, and the great enemy, death, looms ever closer. It is not surprising that many presume the over-65 years to be the worst of times.
20 But, they are not, as Ronald Inglehart (1990) discovered when he amassed interviews conducted during the 1980s with representative samples of nearly 170,000 people from 16
25 nations. Older people report as much happiness and satisfaction with life as younger people do (Figure 4.4).

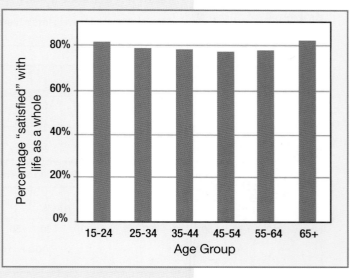

Fig. 4.4 Satisfaction with life of different age groups

Source: Inglehart, R.

If anything, positive feelings grow after midlife and negative feelings subside (Charles & others, 2001; Mroczek, 2001). Older adults increasingly use words that convey positive emotions (Pennebaker &
30 Stone, 2003). They attend less and less to negative information. For example, they are slower than younger adults to perceive negative faces (Mather & Carstense, 2003). Their amygdala, a neural processing center for emotions, shows diminishing activity in response to negative events while maintaining its responsiveness to positive events
35 (Mather & others, 2004). Moreover, the bad feelings we associate with negative events fade faster than do the good feelings we associate with

positive events (Walker et al., 2003). This contributes to most older people's sense that life, on balance, has been mostly good. Given that growing older is an outcome of living (an outcome nearly all of us 40 prefer to early dying), the positivity of later life is comforting.

Compensating for loss

Of course, there are often problems that accompany aging. **Sensory capacities** are not what they used to be. Sight, sense of smell, and hearing all start to decline significantly after the age of 70 (see Figure 4.5). Many **cognitive abilities** also suffer with age. There is memory 45 loss, and there is no doubt that mental speed is lost. However, the brain has a great capacity to compensate for loss.

sensory capacities the ability to see, hear, and smell

cognitive abilities the ability to reason, remember, and solve problems

Fig. 4.5 Graphs showing loss of sensory capacities by age in years

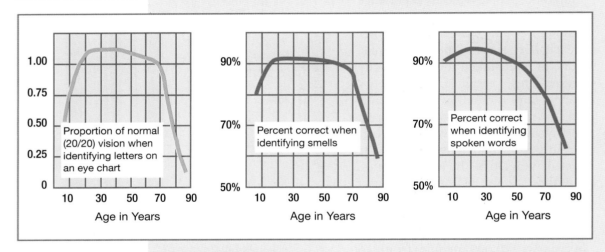

Source: David Meyers

There are other compensations, too. Children have long since "left the nest." They have gone off to school or married and had their own families, but they are still in touch, and now there are grandchildren 50 with whom to interact. Moreover, the children of the elderly have themselves now reached adulthood and are more able and likely to provide support for aging parents.

Although many individuals dread retirement, most in fact welcome it as an opportunity to do those things that they have planned on for 55 years. Retirement also often leads people over 65 to become more physically active after having been in a job where they perhaps had been tied to a desk all day long.

Attitude towards death

Erikson's final stage of psychosocial development is reserved for the period beyond the age of 65. According to Erikson, it is at this stage
60 that it is common for individuals to pause and reflect on their lives, what they have accomplished, the mark they have left, and what they might do with the time remaining. If all goes well with this self-examination, the individual develops a sense of ego identity – a sense of wholeness, an acceptance that all is well and can only get better.
65 If self-examination results in regret, if life seems unfulfilled, with choices badly made, then one may face despair and turn only to death.

Although elderly people may have to deal with dying and death, they are generally less morbid about it than are adolescents. In one study, adults over 60 did more frequently think about and talk about
70 death than did younger adults surveyed. However, of all the adults in the study, the oldest group expressed the least fear of death, some even saying they were eager for it.

Do You Want to Live to Be 100?

Centenarians are people who live to be 100 years old and older. All over the world their numbers are increasing rapidly. Nowhere is this more true than in Japan, where the number of centenarians increased in a six-year period from 20,000 in 2003 to over 40,000 in 2009. The Japanese revere their elderly and even have a weekly television show that profiles a different centenarian each week.

One of the most remarkable Japanese centenarians was surely Keizo Miura. On his 100th birthday, he celebrated by skiing down a mountain in Utah, U.S.A. The year before, to celebrate his 99th birthday, he skied the highest mountain in Europe, Mont Blanc. His son is pretty remarkable too. At the age of 70, he became the oldest man to climb Mount Everest, and in 2013, he plans to go back and climb it again at age 80.

Not everyone, it seems, wants to live to be 100. Research in the United States, which has the highest number of centenarians in the world, has found that the age that most people would like to live to is 87. Most people apparently fear that if they get to be too old, the quality of their life would deteriorate too much. They also fear becoming too much of a burden to their children and grandchildren.

1 Comprehension after speed reading ®

A Write the time it took you to read the text in minutes or fractions of a minute on Line a, (e.g., 7.2 minutes). Divide the number of words by the number of minutes and write the answer on Line c. This is your words per minute reading speed for this reading.

a. time to read in minutes _____

b. number of words ___699___

c. wpm (b/a) _____

d. number correct _____

e. percent correct (dx10) _____

B Now test your understanding of this text by answering these multiple-choice comprehension questions without looking back at the text. Choose the best answer from the choices listed. Have your teacher check your answers and then fill in Lines d and e above. If you are reading at speed, a good goal is to get 70 percent of your answers correct. If you get 100 percent correct, you are either a genius or you are reading too carefully!

1. A good title for this text would be ___ .
   a. Old Age Is Not So Bad After All
   b. The Misery of Old Age
   c. The Joys of Old Age

2. The proportion of elderly people in the population is increasing because ___ .
   a. people are living longer
   b. couples are having fewer children
   c. both *a* and *b*

3. The level of happiness and satisfaction in old age ___ .
   a. is about the same as younger people's
   b. is significantly higher than younger people's
   c. is significantly lower than younger people's

4. The brain of an older person tends to ___ .
   a. notice negative events around them rather than positive ones
   b. more quickly forget the negative things that happen and remember the positive ones
   c. more quickly forget the positive things that happen and remember the negative ones

5. When older people look back on their lives, ___ .
   a. they generally think that their lives have been good
   b. they don't really remember too many details
   c. they have many regrets and wish that they had lived life differently

6. Sensory capacities in old age ___ .
   a. stay about the same
   b. decline significantly
   c. decline slightly

7. One compensation for the elderly that is mentioned in this text is that the elderly ___ .
   a. can look forward to the excitement of remarriage
   b. can afford to pay people to look after them
   c. often have children who can give them financial and practical support

8. According to the text, it is not unusual for people who have had desk jobs to ___ after they retire.
   a. develop serious health problems
   b. take up sedentary hobbies (hobbies you do while sitting)
   c. become much more active

9. Erikson states that in late adulthood we examine our lives and may develop a sense of *ego identity.* This happens when ___ .
   a. we feel bad about our lives and wish we had made better decisions
   b. we feel good about our lives and look to the future with optimism
   c. all we can think about is that we must face death

10. Which of the following statements about elderly people and death is true?
    a. They tend to think about death less than young adults.
    b. They tend to be less afraid of dying than young adults.
    c. They tend to talk about death less frequently than young adults.

2 Describing change ®

English has many different verbs that have subtle differences in meaning. Some of these verbs may be very uncommon, so it is usually not necessary to learn these differences, only to remember their general meaning.

A In this reading, there are several verbs that describe some sort of change of state or size. Look in the text for the verbs on the left, which are given with their subjects. Then match them to the closest meaning on the right.

___ 1. income shrinks   a. get(s) less frequent

___ 2. the body deteriorates   b. get(s) closer and bigger

___ 3. memories fade   c. get(s) less powerful

___ 4. energy wanes   d. get(s) less and less and then stops

___ 5. death looms   e. get(s) less clear, bright, or vivid

___ 6. negative feelings subside   f. get(s) smaller in size

___ 7. activity diminishes   g. get(s) in a worse condition

B Look in the dictionary to see the more precise meaning of each verb in Part A.

C Complete the following sentences with the most appropriate verb from Part A. Use the correct verb form and tense.

1. The political situation in Western Africa is _____ rapidly. Soon there will be no law and order there.

2. Be careful how you wash that shirt. It may _____ .

3. After a while, the shaking from the earthquake began to _____ .

4. We are slowly _____ natural resources by consuming so much.

5. Over time, if you leave an area of carpet exposed to sunlight for too long, it will begin to _____ .

3 Paraphrasing Ⓦ Ⓡ

Sometimes you paraphrase so that you can use someone else's ideas in your essay writing (see Paraphrasing on page 80). However, when you read an important or difficult piece of text, it is also a good idea to try to paraphrase it to get a deeper understanding of it. By rewriting it, you prove to yourself that you have really understood it. This will also help you later if you have to recall the ideas from the text in a test.

A Study this paraphrase of Paragraph 2. Work with a partner and make a list of the changes.

In a study involving approximately 170,000 people from 16 countries, researcher Ronald Inglehart found that there was not much difference between the happiness and satisfaction felt by older and younger people. This may come as a surprise to many people, who believe that after about the age of 65, most elderly people must have miserable lives. They point out that these people have less money to spend, can't get work when they want to, suffer from poor heath, have poor memories, and have less energy than they used to have. Further, they assume that death is never very far from the elderly's thoughts because they have probably already seen some of their friends and family die.

B Reread page 80 to remind yourself of what steps to take when paraphrasing and how to paraphrase appropriately. Work with a partner and write a paraphrase of Paragraph 8.

C Work alone and write a paraphrase of Paragraph 6.

D Compare your paraphrase with a partner's. Notice the differences. Choose one of your paraphrases and work together to improve it.

4 Personalizing the topic Ⓡ

Read the boxed text "Do You Want to Live to Be 100?" and answer the following questions with your class.

1. Do you know of a famous centenarian who is very active in your country or culture? Talk about the person and why he or she is famous.

2. Do you personally know any elderly people who are very active? Talk about who they are and what they do.

3. Would you want to live to be 100? Why or why not?

5 Group projects Ⓐ Ⓡ Ⓦ

> Group projects are a fairly recent instructional tool in college classes. They are seen as developing a key twenty-first-century skill – the ability to work well in teams to solve problems. In a group project, the instructor typically assigns a particular topic to each group and asks the group to research it, write up a group report, and make a group presentation, often using PowerPoint. The group will receive a group grade for their project, so each group member needs to work hard and make sure that other group members work hard, too.

Throughout this unit, the name of Erik Erikson has been mentioned since Erikson is an influential thinker in the field of developmental psychology. Imagine your instructor has given you an assignment to work in groups and research the last four stages of Erikson's theory of psychosocial development, write up a group report, and make a presentation of each stage. Follow the steps below.

A Get into groups of four. Look back through Unit 2 and help each other find every mention of Erikson and his theory.

B Plan how you would divide up the assignment. Which student or students would do each of the following parts of the assignment?

- Do the research
- Write up the report
- Edit the report
- Make the PowerPoint slides
- Make the presentation to the class

C As a class, talk about doing group assignments. If you have done group assignments in the past, talk about how you feel about doing them. Discuss how you feel about getting a group grade for an assignment, rather than an individual grade. Discuss what you think the benefits of group projects are and what the problems are.

Chapter 4 Academic Vocabulary Review

The following are some of the words that appear in Chapter 4. They all come from the Academic Word List, a list of words that researchers have discovered occur frequently in many different types of academic texts. If you can learn these words, it should help you when you have a reading in almost any academic discipline. For a complete list of all the Academic Word List words in this chapter and in all the other readings in this book, see the Appendix on pages 213–214.

Reading 1 Early Adulthood	Reading 2 Middle Adulthood	Reading 3 Late Adulthood
attain	concept	attitude
cite	diminish	challenges
contradiction	dominate	compensate
devote	framework	outcome
emerge	shift (v)	perceive
stability	trigger	presume

Complete the following sentences with words from the lists above.

1. In recent years, there has been a _____ toward postponing marriage.

2. Saying that the elderly have slower mental speed, but greater overall knowledge is not a _____ .

3. It is difficult to _____ that someone is aging.

4. Problems sometimes _____ when we try to do too much.

5. In many cultures, the older you get, the higher the status you _____ .

6. Sometimes a poor test result from your doctor is the only _____ you need to change your dietary habits.

7. The _____ of generativity is a difficult one to understand.

8. Many people _____ that young people are always in good health and optimistic about life.

9. His theory provides a _____ for understanding the different stages of life.

10. It's important to always try to maintain a positive _____ even when things seem to be going badly.

11. The middle years of life are often a time of calm and _____ .

12. Sometimes the brain is able to _____ for the loss of one sense by developing another.

Practicing
Academic Writing

In Unit 2, you have learned about four different stages of life from adolescence to late adulthood. You have studied the characteristics, challenges, and pleasures of each stage. Use this information to write an essay on the topic below.

Two of Life's Stages

Write an essay comparing and contrasting two consecutive periods of life: adolescence and early adulthood, early adulthood and middle adulthood, or middle adulthood and late adulthood. In the essay, clearly describe the main characteristics of the two stages and indicate what you see as being the main challenges and pleasures of each. In your essay, also state which stage you think is the preferable stage of life to be in, and why.

PREPARING TO WRITE

1 Freewriting

Many writers have a problem getting started on their writing assignments. They are afraid that they will have nothing to say. One way to overcome this fear is to do freewriting at the very beginning of the writing process. When you do freewriting, you don't stop and think about what you are writing. You set a time limit, between 5 and 10 minutes, and you write as much as you can as fast as you can. You don't worry about grammar or spelling. Just keep writing. As an idea comes to you, put it down. When another idea comes, write it down. You don't have to be neat and organized; you just have to keep writing.

At the end of this process, you'll be surprised. You will look back at what you have written and you will find one or two ideas and one or two phrases that you will be able to use in your essay. It will get you started. Remember that freewriting is only for you to see, so don't show it to anyone else. And certainly, don't show it to your teacher!

A At the top of a piece of paper, write down the four stages of life: *adolescence*, *early adulthood*, *middle adulthood*, and *late adulthood*. Give yourself a time limit of between 5 and 10 minutes, and start writing. As you write, remember what you know about these periods. Describe them. Compare them. Contrast them. Write about people you know who are in these periods of life or who have been through them. Write about how you feel about these periods of life.

B Look back at what you wrote. Circle three or four ideas and three or four phrases that you think you could develop in to an essay.

C Decide which two periods of life you are going to write about.

2 Read the assignment carefully

> Many students get poor grades on their writing assignments because they don't read the assignment carefully. Always make sure that you understand exactly what is required to complete the essay assignment. If you are not sure, don't be shy. Ask your instructor to explain anything that is unclear to you.

A Read the writing assignment for this unit carefully. How many parts are there to this assignment? Discuss with a partner.

B Create a chart similar to the one below. Write down the names of the two periods of life that you are going to compare and contrast.

C Skim through the readings that are about these periods. As you skim, fill in the chart with ideas that you might be able to use in your essay.

	Period 1:	Period 2:
Main Characteristics		
Pleasures		
Challenges		

D Remember that your assignment asks you to decide which period of life you find preferable. Look through the chart above and decide which period it is going to be.

E Go back through the readings in the unit one more time. Find passages and sections to paraphrase. Look back at the section on Paraphrasing on page 80. Then write your paraphrases, following the guidelines and making sure that you do not plagiarize.

Structuring a comparison-contrast essay

There are two main ways that you can structure a comparison-contrast essay. In the first way, the block method, you write about several different topics relating to item A and then write about the same topics for item B. As you write about B, you make comparisons and contrasts between A and B. In the second method, the switching method, you write on each topic and keep switching from talking about A to talking about B in each section.

Block Method	Switching Method
Introduction	Introduction
Topic 1 about item A	Topic 1 about item A
Topic 2 about item A	Topic 1 about item B
Topic 3 about item A	Topic 2 about item A
Topic 1 about item B	Topic 2 about item B
Topic 2 about item B	Topic 3 about item A
Topic 3 about item B	Topic 3 about item B
Conclusion	Conclusion

A Review your freewriting, the chart you created on page 106, and your paraphrases. Sort through the different ideas you could write about. Then formulate your thesis. (See The Parts of an Essay on pages 26–27 for discussion of a thesis and thesis statements.)

B Write an introductory paragraph that gives the reader some background information about the two periods that you have chosen to compare and contrast.

C At the end of your introduction, write a thesis statement that prepares the reader for the body of your essay and the different ideas that you are going to include.

D Decide which type of structure you are going to give your essay: Block Method or Switching Method. Then make a brief outline of the body of your essay.

E Write the rest of your essay. Remember, a first draft does not have to be perfect. A first draft is just a beginning point. It provides you with some text that you can change until you are satisfied with the final product.

Revising and editing

Revising and editing should not just happen once. Read your essay many times. Every time you read it, you will keep finding places where you can make changes and improve it.

A Read through your essay or ask a friend to read through it. You or your friend should look for things that are unclear, confusing, or unconvincing. Use your friend's feedback to help you revise.

B Answer the following questions to check to see if your essay has the parts of a standard academic essay. Make changes in your second draft if it doesn't.

  1. *Did you include a thesis statement in your introductory paragraph?*
    Check to see that you have a thesis statement that prepares the reader for the body of the essay.

  2. *Did you include topic sentences with your body paragraphs?*
    Check your body paragraphs to see if you have written a general opening statement that prepares the reader for your ideas in the rest of the paragraph.

  3. *Did you support your topic sentences well?*
    Check to see if you have enough details to make the reader feel that your topic sentences are true. If not, add more details to make your ideas more convincing.

  4. *Did you write a conclusion to your essay?*
    Check to see if you wrote a conclusion that reminds the reader of your thesis.

C Read through your essay to edit it.

  1. Look back at Task 3, Synonyms (page 76) and Task 2, Describing Change (page 101). Have you varied your language by using synonyms instead of repeating the same words? Have you used different verbs to describe change? Find places where you can vary the language in your essay.

  2. Look back at Task 3, Hedging (page 67). Are some of your statements too certain? Should you use some hedging language when there is not 100 percent certainty? Find places in your essay where it might be better to use language such as *might*, *can*, *possibly*, *it is likely that*, and so on.

  3. Read through your essay now for possible spelling mistakes, punctuation errors, subject-verb agreement errors, and incorrect use of past tense and articles. Make corrections whenever you find errors.

Unit 3
Nonverbal Messages

In this unit, you will examine the ways in which people communicate nonverbally. In Chapter 5, you will study the ways in which you use your hands, face, and eyes to create meaningful nonverbal messages. In Chapter 6, you will see that the ways you touch and the distances you create between yourself and others also carry messages. The final reading in the chapter focuses on how nonverbal communication can vary from culture to culture.

Contents

In Unit 3, you will read and write about the following topics.

Chapter 5 Body Language	Chapter 6 Touch, Space, and Culture
Reading 1 Gestural Communication	**Reading 1** The Meanings of Touch
Reading 2 Facial Communication	**Reading 2** Spatial Messages
Reading 3 Eye Communication	**Reading 3** Nonverbal Communication and Culture

Skills

In Unit 3, you will practice the following skills.

R Reading Skills

Thinking about the topic
Thinking of your own examples
Thinking critically
Skimming
Personalizing the topic
Increasing reading speed
Comprehension after speed reading
Reading for details
Gathering data
Predicting

W Writing Skills

Defining language
Signaling examples
Paraphrasing
The passive voice
Summarizing
Using adverbs
Generalizations about groups of people
Transitional expressions

V Vocabulary Skills

Words related to the topic
Guessing meaning from context
Ways of looking
Word families
Collocations

A Academic Success Skills

Outlining practice
Highlighting
Taking notes
Exploring key concepts
Writing short answers to test questions
Making a chart
Answering a short-answer test question
Synthesizing

Learning Outcomes

Produce a handbook that will help someone who is not a member of your culture understand how your culture uses body language.

Previewing the Unit

Before reading a unit (or chapter) of a textbook, it is a good idea to preview the contents page and think about the topics that will be covered. This will give you an overview of how the unit is organized and what it is going to be about.

Read the contents page for Unit 3 on page 110 and do the following activities.

Chapter 5: Body Language

A With a partner, make a list of the different elements of body language. Decide which one you think is the single most powerful element. Be prepared to defend your decision to the rest of the class with examples.

B Researchers in nonverbal communication often claim that our body language can influence people's impressions of us more than the words we use. Body language can determine how well or badly an interaction with another person goes. With a partner, think of three different situations – with friends and family, or in a business, educational, or medical interaction – in which a person's body language might have a strong impact on what happens. Be prepared to describe your situations to the rest of the class.

Chapter 6: Touch, Space, and Culture

A In Chapter 6, you will read that the amount that people touch each other varies greatly from culture to culture. Is yours a "high-contact culture" (people touch a lot) or a "low-contact" one? Explain.

B In "Spatial Messages," you will read about the different distances we usually keep between ourselves and others. Look at the diagram. Imagine that it represents the only free table and chairs in the school cafeteria. All the chairs at this table are empty except the one marked X. Where would you sit if the person seated in X was:

1. someone to whom you are attracted and would like to date, but to whom you have never spoken?

2. your boyfriend or girlfriend, with whom you are in love?

3. a favorite instructor whom you would like to get to know better?

4. an instructor who gave you an undeserved F in a course and whom you dislike intensely?

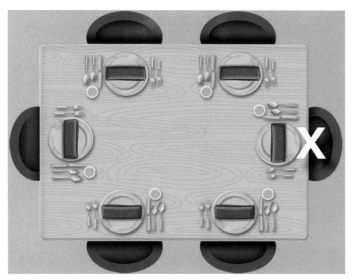

Chapter 5
Body Language

Thinking about the topic ®

In this text, you are going to read about a classification of gestures into five different types:

emblems   illustrators   affect displays   regulators   adaptors

The five pairs of situations in the table below illustrate the five different types of gestures. Before you read, work with a partner and show each other what gesture you might make in each situation. After you read the text, fill in the table with the name of the type of gesture.

What would you do . . . ?	Type of gesture
1a. to show someone that you are very angry with her 1b. to show someone that you think what she just said was absolutely amazing	
2a. to show someone that you are listening very carefully to what he is saying to you 2b. to show someone that you have finished speaking and now you want him to respond in some way	
3a. to show someone that what she just did was perfect, just great 3b. to show someone that you think another person, perhaps across the room, is absolutely crazy	
4a. if you were sitting alone and you had an itch on your chin 4b. if your lips were dry and you needed to moisten them	
5a. if you were telling someone that you caught a big fish 5b. if you were explaining to someone how you caught a ball	

Reading 1

GESTURAL COMMUNICATION

Introduction

Nonverbal communication is communication without words. You communicate nonverbally when you gesture, smile or frown, widen your eyes, move your chair closer to someone, wear jewelry, touch someone, or raise your
5 vocal volume, even when you say nothing.

Your ability to use nonverbal communication effectively can yield two major benefits. First, the greater your ability to send and receive nonverbal signals, the higher your attraction, popularity, and
10 psychosocial well-being are likely to be. Second, the greater your nonverbal skills, the more successful you are likely to be in a wide variety of interpersonal communication situations, including business communication, teacher-student communication, intercultural communication, courtroom
15 communication, and in close relationships, politics, and health care.

In this unit, we will look at five different channels of nonverbal communication: (1) gestural communication, (2) facial communication, (3) eye communication, (4) touch communication, and (5) spatial messages. We begin our study of nonverbal messages by considering
20 gestural communication.

Types of gestures

An especially useful classification in **kinesics**, the study of communication through body movement, identifies five types of gestures: emblems, illustrators, affect displays, regulators,
25 and adaptors.

kinesics the study of human body movements

Emblems

Emblems are substitutes for words; they are body movements that have rather specific translations, such as the nonverbal signs for "OK,"
30 "Peace," "Come here," "Go away," "Who, me?" "Be quiet," "I'm warning you," "I'm tired," and "It's cold." Emblems are as

arbitrary as any words in any language. Consequently, your present
35 culture's emblems are not necessarily the same as your culture's
emblems of 300 years ago or the same as the emblems of other cultures.
For example, the sign made by forming a circle with the thumb and
the forefinger may mean "nothing" or "zero" in France, "money" in
Japan, and something sexual in certain southern European cultures.
40 But, just as the English language is spreading throughout the world,
so too is the English nonverbal language. The American use of this
emblem to mean "OK" is spreading just as fast as, for example, English
technical and scientific terms.

Illustrators

Illustrators accompany and literally illustrate verbal messages.
45 Illustrators make your communications more vivid and help to
maintain your listener's attention. They also help to clarify and
intensify your verbal messages. In saying, "Let's go up," for example,
you probably move your head and perhaps your finger in an upward
direction. In describing a circle or a square, you more than likely
50 make circular or square movements with your hands. Research points
to another advantage of illustrators: They increase your ability to
remember. People who illustrated their verbal messages with gestures
remembered about 20 percent more than those who did not gesture.

We are aware of illustrators only part of the time; at times they may
55 have to be brought to our attention and our awareness. Illustrators are
more universal than emblems; they will be recognized and understood
by members of more cultures than will emblems.

Affect displays

Affect displays are the movements of the facial area that convey emotional
meaning – the expressions that show anger and fear, happiness and
60 surprise, and eagerness and fatigue. They are the facial expressions that
show your true feelings when you are trying to present a false image
and that lead people to say, "You look angry. What's wrong?" We can,
however, consciously control affect displays, as actors do when they play
a role. Affect displays may be unintentional (as when they show your
65 true feelings), or intentional (as when you want to show anger or love).

Regulators

Regulators monitor, maintain, or control the speaking of another
individual. When you listen to another, you are not passive; you nod
your head, purse your lips, adjust your eye focus, and make various
paralinguistic sounds, such as "mm-mm" or "tsk." Regulators are
70 culture-bound: Each culture develops its own rules for the regulation

of conversation. Regulators also include such broad movements as shaking your head to show disbelief or leaning forward in your chair to show that you want to hear more.

Regulators communicate what you expect or want speakers
75 to do as they are talking; for example, "Keep going," "Tell me what happened," "I don't believe that. Are you sure?" "Speed up," and "Slow down." Speakers often receive these nonverbal behaviors without being consciously aware of them. Depending on their degree of sensitivity, speakers modify their speaking behavior in accordance
80 with these regulators.

Adaptors

Adaptors satisfy some need and usually occur without conscious awareness; they are unintentional movements that usually go unnoticed. Researchers identify three main types of adaptors based on their focus, direction, or target:
85 self-adaptors, alter-adaptors, and object-adaptors.

Self-adaptors usually satisfy a physical need, generally serving to make you more comfortable; examples include scratching your head to relieve an itch, moistening your lips because they feel
90 dry, or pushing your hair out of your eyes. When these adaptors occur in private, they occur in their entirety: You scratch your head until the itch is gone. But in public, these adaptors usually occur in abbreviated form.
95 When people are watching you, for example, you might put your fingers to your head and move them around a bit but probably not scratch with the same vigor as when in private.

Alter-adaptors are the body movements you make
100 in response to your current interactions. Examples include crossing your arms over your chest when someone unpleasant approaches or moving closer to someone you like.

Object-adaptors are movements that involve your manipulation of some object. Frequently observed examples include punching holes
105 in or drawing on a piece of paper, clicking a ballpoint pen, or chewing on a pencil. Object-adaptors are usually signs of negative feelings; for example, you emit more adaptors when you feel hostile than when you feel friendly. Further, as anxiety and uneasiness increase, so does the frequency of object-adaptors.

Scratching one's head is an example of a self-adaptor.

1 Outlining practice Ⓐ Ⓦ

> Sometimes it is a good idea to create a simple skeleton outline of a text so that you can get a clear idea of its structure. The outline will help you later if you need to go back and put in more details to study the text for a test.

A Complete the following skeleton outline of "Gestural Communication."

  I. Introduction
    A. Definition of Nonverbal Communication (NVC):
       Communication without words
    B. Reasons it is important to be able to use NVC effectively
       1. _____
       2. _____
  II. Types of Gestures
    A. Emblems
    B. _____
    C. _____
    D. _____
    E. _____
       1. self-adaptors
       2. _____
       3. _____

B Compare your outline with a partner's.

2 Highlighting Ⓐ

> Remember, when you highlight a text it is a good idea to use several different colors systematically. For example, use one color for definitions of key terms and a second color for examples of these terms.

A Find definitions of the following terms in this text and highlight them in the same color.

emblems	**illustrators**	**affect displays**	**regulators**
adaptors	**self-adaptors**	**alter-adaptors**	**object-adaptors**

B Find examples of each of the different gesture types and highlight them in a different color.

C Following the definition and examples of each gesture type, the author sometimes adds some observations or commentary. Find these observations and commentary and highlight them in a third color. For example, in the part of the text on emblems, you would highlight the following observations and commentary.

Emblems are . . . arbitrary

Consequently, your present culture's emblems are not necessarily the same as your culture's emblems of 300 years ago or the same as the emblems of other cultures.

. . . just as the English language is spreading throughout the world, so too is the English nonverbal language.

D Compare answers with a partner's and see if you have highlighted the same definitions, examples, and commentary.

3 Taking notes Ⓐ Ⓡ

Notes should be brief, complete, and easy to read. Below are some useful guidelines for how to take effective notes; however, ultimately you may want to develop a system of note-taking that works for you.

- Use abbreviations and symbols, but make sure you will know what they mean when you look at them later.
- Do not crowd your notes. Make them easy to read by leaving plenty of space around them.
- Make sure main points stand out by (1) underlining and numbering them, (2) indenting lower-level details (as in an outline), and (3) leaving space between each main point.
- Write legibly.

A Look at how one student took notes for the part of the text under the heading "Emblems." Work with a partner. Without looking back at the text, and working from these notes only, explain this section of the text.

> 1. Emblems
>   - Def. = nonverb. behaviors that translate words or phrases
>   Ex – OK, Peace, Come here, etc.
>   - Arbitrary
>   - Embs diff. in diff. times + cults
>   Ex - OK sign = 0 in France, = money in Japan, = sexual
>   meaning in some s. Euro countries
>   - Engl. embs spreading in world, e.g., OK sign

B Take notes on another part of the text. Use your own note-taking system. Then, using only your notes, work with a partner and give an oral summary of that part.

4 Defining language Ⓦ Ⓥ

A common way to define a term is to use the following sentence structure:
plural noun + *are* + plural noun + *that* + present tense verb

A Notice the way that *emblems* is defined in this reading:

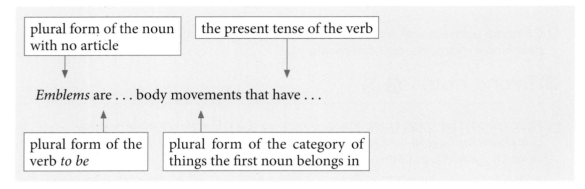

| plural form of the noun with no article | the present tense of the verb |

Emblems are . . . body movements that have . . .

| plural form of the verb *to be* | plural form of the category of things the first noun belongs in |

B Look at the definition of the other seven terms that you highlighted in Task 2. Which of them are defined in the same way as *emblems*?

C The four terms not defined in the same way as *emblems* can easily be defined that way. Rewrite them using the formula.

5 Signaling examples Ⓦ Ⓡ

Look at some different ways that writers introduce or "signal" that they are giving the reader examples.

| **for example** | **for instance** | **such as** | **an example of X is** |
| **including** | **X include(s)** | **examples include** | |

In a text that contains a large number of examples, you can expect the writer to vary his or her language and use several different ways to signal them. When you write a text with a lot of examples, vary your language too.

A Look back at the examples that you highlighted in Task 2. Find and circle any language that signals the examples. How many different types of signals did you find?

B Writers don't always start an example with a signal. Underline places in the text where examples follow the definition without a signal.

6 Thinking of your own examples Ⓡ Ⓦ

One way that you can demonstrate to yourself that you have really understood a text is to see if you can come up with your own examples.

A Work with a partner and think of one or two of your own examples of the different types of gestures below. Make notes.

- Emblems
- Illustrators
- Affect Displays
- Regulators
- Self-Adaptors

B From your notes, write three sentences about each type of gesture. The first sentence is a definition and the second and third sentences use your own examples. Use the defining language from Task 4 for the first sentence and the signaling language from Task 5 for the second and third sentences.

C Share your examples with the class by reading out your sentences.

7 Thinking critically Ⓡ

Testing a key concept or hypothesis in a text can help you think critically about what you have read and help you to develop a greater understanding of the concept.

A According to this text, not all cultures use the same emblem gestures. Test this idea by asking people from different cultures to show you what gestures they would make in order to communicate the following:

I am sleepy.	Please forgive me.
I am broke.	Good luck.
I have no idea.	Come here.
I am thinking.	Good-bye.
I am hungry.	You are late.

B Think of an emblem gesture used in your country that you think may have a different meaning in another country. Make the gesture and ask classmates who come from a different country what it means.

C Discuss whether you see any evidence that American nonverbal language is spreading throughout the world.

1 Skimming ®

Quickly skim "Facial Communication." In which sections can you read the following ideas? Write *1*, *2*, or *3* on the line depending on whether the idea is in Section 1, 2, or 3 of the reading.

Section 1: Facial Expressions

Section 2: Facial Management

Section 3: Facial Feedback

_____ **a.** Some facial expressions are easier to interpret than others.

_____ **b.** People adjust their facial expressions to be socially acceptable.

_____ **c.** An expression on someone's face can affect how they feel.

_____ **d.** People may alter their facial expressions in different interpersonal situations.

_____ **e.** Context can affect how people interpret a facial expression.

2 Words related to the topic ⓥ

Sometimes in a reading you will encounter topic-related words that all belong to the same group. You may need to learn this group of words and the differences between them.

A This text refers to a number of emotional states that the face can express. Work with a partner. Share the meanings of the words you know and find out the meanings of any words that neither of you know.

happiness _____	disgust _____
surprise _____	contempt _____
fear _____	interest _____
anger _____	bewilderment _____
sadness _____	determination _____

B Define the states from Activity A using the following language:

X is an emotional state that you feel when *Y* occurs.

C Write the adjective forms of these words on the lines in Activity A. Use a dictionary to help you if necessary.

Reading 2

FACIAL COMMUNICATION

Facial expressions

Throughout your interpersonal interactions your face communicates, especially signaling your emotions. In fact, facial movements alone seem to communicate the degree of pleasantness, agreement, and sympathy a person feels; the rest of the body doesn't provide any
5 additional information. For other aspects, however – for example, the intensity with which an emotion is felt – both facial and bodily cues are used.

Some nonverbal-communication researchers claim that facial movements may communicate at least the following eight emotions:
10 happiness, surprise, fear, anger, sadness, disgust, contempt, and interest. Others propose that, in addition, facial movements may communicate bewilderment and determination.

Of course, some emotions are easier to communicate than others. For example, in one study, happiness was judged with an accuracy
15 ranging from 55 percent to 100 percent, surprise from 38 percent to 86 percent, and sadness from 19 percent to 88 percent. Research finds that women and girls are more accurate judges of facial emotional expressions than men and boys.

As you have probably experienced, you may interpret the same
20 facial expressions differently depending on the context in which they occur. For example, in a classic study, when a smiling face was presented looking at a glum face, the smiling face was judged to be vicious. But when the same smiling face was presented looking at a frowning face, it was judged to be peaceful and friendly. In general, not
25 surprisingly, people who smile are judged to be more likable and more approachable than people who don't smile or people who pretend to smile. And women perceive men who are smiled at by other women as being more attractive than men who are not smiled at. But men – perhaps being more competitive – perceive men whom women smile
30 at as being less attractive than men who are not smiled at.

Facial management

In the same way that you learned the nonverbal system of communication unconsciously as a child, you also learned certain facial management techniques that enable you to communicate your feelings to achieve the effect you want – for example, to hide certain
35 emotions and to emphasize others. Consider your own use of such facial techniques. As you do so, think about when you might do the following:

- *Intensify* your facial expression, as when you exaggerate your surprise when friends throw you a surprise party.
- *Deintensify* your facial expression, as when you cover up your own joy in the presence of a friend who didn't receive such good news.
- *Neutralize* your facial expression, as when you cover up your sadness to keep from depressing others.
- *Mask* your facial expression, as when you express happiness in order to cover up your disappointment at not receiving the gift you expected.

These facial management techniques help you display emotions in socially acceptable ways. For example, when someone gets bad news about which you secretly take pleasure, the display rules dictate that you frown and otherwise nonverbally signal your sorrow. If you place first in a race and your best friend barely finishes, the display rules require that you minimize your expression of pleasure in winning and avoid signs of gloating. If you violate these display rules, you'll be judged as insensitive. So, although facial management techniques may be deceptive, they are also expected – and, in fact, required by the rules of polite interaction.

Facial feedback

facial feedback hypothesis
the theory that your facial expressions affect your emotions (as well as the reverse)

When you express emotions facially, a feedback effect is observed. This finding has given rise to the **facial feedback hypothesis**, which holds that your facial expressions influence your own physiological arousal. For example, in one study, participants held a pen in their teeth to simulate a sad expression and then rated a series of photographs. Results showed that mimicking a sad expression actually increased the degree of sadness the subjects reported when viewing the photographs.

Generally, research finds that facial expressions can produce or heighten feelings of sadness, fear, disgust, and anger. But this effect does not occur with all emotions; smiling, for example, won't make you feel happier. And if you're feeling sad, smiling is not likely to replace your sadness with happiness. A reasonable conclusion seems to be that your facial expressions can influence some feelings, but not others.

70

Can You Tell from a Facial Expression if Someone Is Lying?

A drama on U.S. television that premiered in 2009 is called *Lie to Me*. The main character is Dr. Cal Lightman, a psychologist who assists law enforcement by helping them find out if someone is lying to them. In the show, Lightman reads people's body language, especially their faces, to tell if they are lying. Can someone really do this?

The character of Dr. Lightman is actually based on a real psychologist, Dr. Paul Ekman, who has been studying facial expressions for over 50 years. He has created a system called M.E.T.T., which stands for Micro Expression Training Tool. According to Ekman, the face produces thousands of tiny movements, or micro expressions, which he has cataloged. His claim is that, if you train people to notice these expressions, which may last for just 1/15 to 1/25 of a second, they can tell if they are being lied to.

Ekman's techniques have been taught to the FBI, the CIA, and other law enforcement agencies Perhaps these trained experts can tell if someone is lying to them, but for most of us, however, there's probably no way to tell at all.

1 Exploring key concepts Ⓐ Ⓥ

When a reading contains a key concept or hypothesis, you can deepen your understanding of the concept by testing it in some way. According to a key hypothesis in this text, certain facial expressions are fairly easy to interpret.

A Find the face that best expresses each emotion and write the letter of that face in the blank. Compare answers with your classmates.

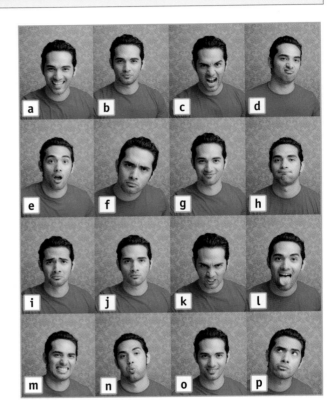

___ **happiness**

___ **anger**

___ **fear**

___ **sadness**

___ **disgust**

___ **interest**

B Work with a partner. Choose one of the emotions listed in Activity A and make a facial expression to show that emotion. See if your partner can guess the emotion from your expression.

2 Guessing meaning from context Ⓥ Ⓡ

It is often possible to get a general idea of the meaning of a word or phrase by looking at its context.

Read these passages from the text and use the context to work out what the words in bold probably mean.

For example, in a classic study, when a smiling face was presented looking at a **glum** face, the smiling face was judged to be **vicious**. But when the same smiling face was presented looking at a **frowning** face, it was judged to be peaceful and friendly.

glum _____

vicious _____

frowning _____

If you place first in a race and your best friend barely finishes, the display rules require that you minimize your expression of pleasure in winning and avoid signs of **gloating**. If you **violate** the display rules, you'll be judged as **insensitive**.

gloating _____

violate _____

insensitive _____

For example, in one study, participants held a pen in their teeth to **simulate** a sad expression and then rated a series of photographs. Results showed that **mimicking** a sad expression actually increased the degree of sadness the **subjects** reported when viewing the photographs.

simulate _____

mimicking _____

subjects _____

Ekman . . . has created a system called M.E.T.T., which **stands for** Micro Expression Training Tool. According to Ekman, the face produces thousands of tiny movements, or micro expressions, which he has **cataloged**. His claim is that, if you train people to notice these expressions, which may **last** for just 1/15 to 1/25 of a second, they can tell if they are being lied to.

stands for _____

cataloged _____

last _____

3 Paraphrasing Ⓦ

> You use paraphrasing when you include someone else's ideas in your own writing. You can also use paraphrasing when you encounter a difficult piece of text. Rewriting the text in your own words is a way to deeply interact with the text as you struggle to understand it. (See page 80 for guidelines on how to paraphrase.)

A Work in groups of three students. One student will take notes on Paragraph 4, the second student on Paragraph 6, and the third student on Paragraph 7.

B Use your notes to tell the other students in your group about your paragraph.

C Write a paraphrase of your paragraph, making sure to change the sentence structure and vocabulary used in the original.

D Share and critique the paraphrases in your group.

4 Personalizing the topic Ⓡ

Answer the following questions in pairs or in small groups.

1. Are you good at "reading" other people's facial expressions? Explain.

2. According to Paragraph 3, women are better at judging the meaning of facial expressions than men. Do you think that is true? Explain why or why not.

3. According to the text, people often "manage" their facial expressions to hide what they are really feeling. Have you ever done the following? Explain the situation and show what you did.

   Have you . . . ?
   - exaggerated a happy expression to make people think you were happier than you really were
   - pretended to be happy when you weren't really
   - covered up your joy so that other people who were not so happy didn't feel bad
   - frowned when someone got bad news and you were secretly pleased

4. In the discussion of the facial feedback hypothesis, the writer states that this hypothesis holds true for some emotions, but not others. For example, smiling won't make you feel happier. Does your experience agree with this hypothesis and this claim? Discuss.

5. Do you think you can tell when people are lying to you? If you do, what sorts of body language signals do you look for to tell if someone might be lying?

1 Ways of looking ⓥ

The following verbal expressions, taken from the text and listed in the left-hand column below, describe "ways of looking." Match each expression on the left with an equivalent expression on the right.

___ **1.** lock eyes with someone

___ **2.** gaze at someone

___ **3.** look at someone intently

___ **4.** glance at someone

___ **5.** catch someone's eye

___ **6.** avert one's glance

___ **7.** make eye contact with someone

a. avoid eye contact with someone by looking away

b. look at someone until they look at you

c. get someone's attention with your eyes

d. look quickly at someone and then look away

e. look at someone with interest or pleasure for a fairly long time

f. stare at someone, perhaps making them feel uncomfortable

g. make eye contact with someone and hold it for a long time

2 Increasing reading speed Ⓡ

Use this text as an opportunity to practice your speed-reading skills. Before you start, review the guidelines for faster reading on page 34 in Chapter 2.

Read the text "Eye Communication" to practice reading for speed. Time yourself. When you finish, turn to the tasks that begin on page 131 and write down how long it took you to read the text.

Reading 3

EYE COMMUNICATION

Occulesis is the study of messages communicated by the eyes. These messages vary depending on the duration, direction, and quality of the eye behavior. For example, in every culture there are rather strict, though unstated, rules for proper duration of **eye contact**. In much of
5 England and the United States, for example, the average length of gaze is 2.95 seconds. The average length of mutual gaze (two persons gazing at each other) is 1.18 seconds. When the duration of eye contact is shorter than 1.18 seconds, you may think the person is uninterested, shy, or preoccupied. When the appropriate amount of time is exceeded,
10 you may perceive this as showing high interest.

eye contact
a speaker and a listener looking directly into each other's eyes

There are rules that govern eye contact. They may vary from culture to culture.

In much of the United States, direct eye contact is considered an expression of honesty and forthrightness. But the Japanese often view eye contact as lack of
15 respect. The Japanese will glance at the other person's face rarely and then only for very short periods. In many Hispanic cultures, direct eye contact signifies a certain equality and so should be avoided
20 by, say, children when speaking to a person in authority. Try visualizing the potential misunderstanding that eye communication alone could create when people from Tokyo, San Francisco, and San Juan try to
25 communicate.

The direction of the eye also communicates. Generally, when communicating with another person, you will glance alternatively at the other person's face, then away, then again at the face, and so on. When these directional rules are broken, different meanings are
30 communicated – abnormally high or low interest, self-consciousness, nervousness over the interaction and so on. The quality of the gaze – how wide or narrow your eyes get during the interaction – also communicates meaning, especially interest level and such emotions as surprise, fear, and disgust.

35 Studies also show that listeners gaze at speakers more than speakers gaze at listeners. The percentage of interaction time spent gazing while listening, for example, ranges from 62 percent to 75 percent; the percentage of time spent gazing while talking, however, ranges from 38 to 41 percent. When these percentages are reversed – when a
40 speaker gazes at the listener for longer than "normal" periods or when the listener gazes at the speaker for shorter than "normal" periods – the conversational interaction becomes awkward.

Eye contact functions

Eye contact serves several important functions.

- *To monitor feedback.* For example, when you talk with others, you look at them intently and try to understand their reaction to what you are saying. You try to read their feedback and, on this basis, you adjust what you say. As you can imagine, successful readings of feedback will help considerably in your overall effectiveness.

- *To secure attention.* When you speak with two or three other people, you maintain eye contact to secure the attention and interest of your listeners. When someone fails to pay you the attention that you want, you probably increase your eye contact, hoping that this will increase attention.

- *To regulate the conversation.* Eye contact helps you regulate, manage, and control the conversation. With eye movements, you can inform the other person that she or he should speak. A clear example of this occurs in the college classroom, where the instructor asks a question and then locks eyes with a student. This type of eye contact tells the student to answer the question.

- *To signal the nature of the relationship.* Eye communication also can serve as a "tie sign" to signal the nature of the relationship between two people – for example, to indicate positive or negative regard. Depending on the culture, eye contact may communicate your romantic interest in another person, or eye avoidance may indicate respect.

- *To signal status.* Eye contact is often used to signal status and aggression. Among younger people, prolonged eye contact from a stranger is taken to signify aggressiveness and frequently prompts physical violence – merely because one person looked perhaps a little longer than was considered normal in that specific culture.

- *To compensate for physical distance.* Eye contact is often used to compensate for increased physical distance. By making eye contact, you overcome psychologically the physical distance between yourself and another person. When you catch someone's eye at a party, for example, you become psychologically close even though you may be separated by a considerable physical distance.

Eye avoidance

The eyes, observed sociologist Erving Goffman in *Interaction Ritual* (1967) are "great intruders." When you avoid eye contact or avert your glance, you allow others to maintain their privacy. You probably do this when you see a couple arguing in the street or on a bus. You turn your eyes away as if to say, "I don't mean to intrude; I respect your privacy." Goffman refers to this behavior as *civil inattention*.

85 Eye avoidance also can signal a lack of interest in a person, a conversation, or some visual stimulus. At times, like the ostrich, you hide your eyes in an attempt to cut off unpleasant stimuli. Notice, for example, how quickly people close their eyes in the face of some extreme unpleasantness. Interestingly enough, even if the

90 unpleasantness is auditory, you tend to shut it out by closing your eyes. Sometimes you close your eyes to block out visual stimuli and thus to heighten your other senses; for example, we often listen to music with our eyes closed. Lovers often close their eyes while kissing and many prefer to make love in a dark or dimly lit room.

Pupil dilation

95 In the fifteenth and sixteenth centuries in Italy, women used to put drops of belladonna (which literally means "beautiful woman") into their eyes to enlarge their pupils so that they would look more attractive. Research in the field of pupillometrics supports the intuitive logic of these women: Dilated pupils are in fact judged to be more

100 attractive than constricted ones.

You may feel differently about the woman in the top photograph than you do about the woman in the bottom one.

In one study, photographs of women were retouched. In one set of photographs, the pupils were enlarged and in another, they were made smaller. Men were then asked to judge the

105 women's personalities from the photographs. The photos of women with small pupils drew responses such as cold, hard, and selfish; those with dilated pupils drew responses such as feminine and soft. However, the male observers

110 could not verbalize the reasons for the different perceptions. Both pupil dilation itself and people's reactions to changes in the pupil size of others seem to function below the level of conscious awareness.

115 Pupil size is also indicative of your interest and level of emotional arousal. Your pupils enlarge when you are interested in something or when you are emotionally aroused. Perhaps we find dilated pupils more attractive because we judge them as indicative of an interest in us.

120 Although belladonna is no longer used, the cosmetics industry has made millions selling eye enhancers such as eye shadow, eyeliner, false eyelashes, and tinted contact lenses that change eye color. These items function (ideally, at least) to draw attention to these powerful communicators.

1 Comprehension after speed reading ®

A Write the time it took you to read the text in minutes or fractions of a minute on Line a (e.g., 7.2 minutes). Divide the number of words by the number of minutes and write the answer on Line c. This is your words per minute reading speed for this reading.

a. time to read in minutes _____

b. number of words ___1156___

c. wpm (b/a) _____

d. number correct _____

e. percent correct (dx10) _____

B Now test your understanding by answering these multiple-choice comprehension questions without looking back at the text. Choose the best answer from the choices listed. Have your teacher check your answers and then fill in Lines d and e above. When reading at speed, a good goal is to get 70 percent of your answers correct. If you get 100 percent correct, you are probably reading too carefully.

1. On average in the United States and England, two people will look into each other's eyes (a mutual gaze) for approximately ___ .
a. half a second
b. one second
c. three seconds

2. According to the text, in Japan, long and direct eye contact is often considered to be ___ .
a. a sign of honesty
b. a sign of disrespect
c. a sign that one is a person of authority

3. Who looks at whom more during a normal interaction?
a. The speaker looks more at the listener.
b. The listener looks more at the speaker.
c. The listener and speaker both look at each other about the same amount.

4. One of the functions of eye contact, as seen in the example of when an instructor looks at a student, is ___ .
a. to show disapproval
b. to show it is the listener's turn to speak
c. to show that you are pleased with someone

5. If you see someone at a party whom you would like to get to know better, and this person makes eye contact with you and then breaks it very quickly, this is ___ .
a. a sign that the person is probably very shy but would like to get to know you
b. a sign that the person is flirting with you
c. a sign that the person is probably not interested in getting to know you

6. We may make more eye contact than normal with someone when ___ .
   a. we are physically a little distant from them
   b. we do not particularly like them
   c. we are standing very close to them

7. One reason for avoiding eye contact is so that ___ .
   a. people will not be able to see what we are thinking
   b. we will be able to listen better to someone's private conversation
   c. we may give someone the sense that we are respecting their privacy

8. We may close our eyes to ___ .
   a. block some unpleasant sensation
   b. be even more aware of a pleasant sensation
   c. do either of the above

9. If a photograph of a woman is changed to make her pupils look larger, men will tend to judge the woman as ___ .
   a. being more attractive
   b. having a colder personality
   c. appearing more selfish

10. What happens to the pupils of the eyes when someone is emotionally aroused?
    a. They become smaller.
    b. They become larger.
    c. They appear to become larger but, in fact, they stay the same size.

2 Writing short answers to test questions Ⓐ Ⓦ

> Since a perfect answer to even a short-answer test question will usually include several pieces of information, be sure to read each question carefully and think about everything that should be included in a correct answer. Decide if a complete answer requires examples. The more complete your answer, the more points your teacher will give.

A Read the following questions about this text and the answers given by one student. If a perfect answer gets 10 points, decide how many points you would give for each of these answers.

1. What is studied in occulesis?
   Occulesis is the study of how messages are communicated with the eyes. In particular, it is concerned with the duration of eye contact.
                        score: ___ points

2. Is eye contact behavior the same in all cultures? Explain your answer.
   No. Eye contact behavior is not the same in all cultures. In some cultures, people make longer eye contact than people in other cultures.
                        score: ___ points

3. One of the six functions of eye contact is to regulate conversation. Explain this function and give an example.

By using eye contact, it is possible to regulate a conversation. For example, you can use eye contact to tell someone that you have finished speaking and they can now speak. Another example is when a college instructor locks eyes with a student. In this case, the eye contact indicates to the student that he or she should answer the question.

score: ___ points

4. What is pupillometrics and what is one finding from this field of study?

In a study of pupil dilation, it was found that people who have large pupils are judged to be more attractive than people who have small pupils.

score: ___ points

5. What does Goffman mean by "civil inattention"?

"Civil inattention" is a type of behavior that occurs when someone turns their eyes away from other people's public conversation, politely showing by not looking that they are trying not to listen.

score: ___ points

B Compare your scores in a small group. Explain why you gave each score. For any answer for which you decided not to give a perfect score, describe how you think the answer could be improved.

C Choose one of the questions above. Close your book and write a short answer. When you have finished writing, give your answer to another student to score (a perfect answer gets 10 points). After you score each other's questions, explain why you gave the score that you did.

Chapter 5 Academic Vocabulary Review

The following are some of the words that appear in Chapter 5. They all come from the Academic Word List, a list of words that researchers have discovered occur frequently in many different types of academic texts. If you can learn these words, it should help you when you have a reading in almost any academic discipline. For a complete list of all the Academic Word List words in this chapter and in all the other readings in this book, see the Appendix on pages 213–214.

Reading 1 Gestural Communication	Reading 2 Facial Communication	Reading 3 Eye Communication
arbitrary clarify consequently maintain manipulation modify	conclusion context hypothesis interaction interpret series	duration exceed function (v) monitor (v) mutual signify

Complete the following sentences with words from the lists above.

1. You could tell by the way they behaved that they had _____ respect for each other.

2. The researcher showed the subjects a _____ of photos with different facial expressions on them.

3. He was really quite sad, so he could not _____ a smile for very long.

4. The researcher realized she had made a serious mistake; _____ she decided to go back and do the experiment again.

5. The number he chose for his password was quite _____ .

6. She was told that her password could not _____ eight numbers.

7. What did his silence _____ . Nobody knew.

8. When you _____ the photograph by making the pupils bigger, people judge the woman to be more attractive.

9. He began his research with a very simple _____ .

10. After his research came to an end, he came to a very simple _____ .

11. The _____ of the gesture was very brief – only about half a second.

12. It was impossible to _____ her emotion from her facial expression.

Developing Writing Skills

In this section, you will learn about and practice summarizing. At the end of the unit, you will be given your essay assignment, in which you will be asked to use information from the readings in the unit. When you include this information in your essay, you will use your summarizing skills.

Summarizing

Summarizing is similar to paraphrasing (see page 80 for guidelines on writing a paraphrase). When you paraphrase, you put a short piece of text into your own words; the paraphrase is usually about the same length as the original and contains the same information as the original. When you summarize, however, you reduce the original text to a much shorter text and only include the most essential information.

You can summarize a paragraph, an article, a chapter, or a whole book. When you summarize a paragraph, you might write a sentence. When you summarize an article or a chapter, you might write a paragraph.

Before you write a summary, it is a good idea to reread the original and take notes. Then write your summary from your notes without looking back at the original until you are finished.

Here are the characteristics of a well-written summary of a longer piece of writing.

1. It should be much shorter than the original.
2. The first sentence should express the overall message of the original text.
3. The remaining sentences should express the main ideas that support the overall message.
4. Detailed information should be avoided.
5. It should be written in your own words, avoiding the exact phrasing and sentence structure of the original.
6. Where you feel you need to use words from the original, put those words in quotation marks.

A Reread Paragraph 2 from "Gestural Communication" on page 113. Which of the sentences below is the best one-sentence summary of this paragraph? After you decide, discuss your reasons for choosing this sentence and rejecting the others.

1. You can get major benefits from being a good nonverbal communicator, including increased popularity, attractiveness, well-being, and success in communicating in business, school, politics, healthcare and personal situations.

2. There are many benefits to being able to communicate effectively nonverbally.

3. If you can use nonverbal communication well, you are more likely to achieve success in both your personal and professional life.

4. Good communicators know how to use both nonverbal and verbal communication effectively.

B Reread the boxed text on page 123 and write a one-sentence summary of it. Compare and critique your summary with a partner. Together, write a one-sentence summary that you both think is effective and share it with the rest of the class.

C Reread "Eye Communication" on pages 128–130. With a partner, decide which of the following sentences best captures the overall message of the text and would serve as a good opening sentence for a summary of the reading.

1. Eye communication is an interesting field of study.

2. The rules of eye communication are different in different cultures.

3. When we look at people for a long time, glance at them quickly, or avoid eye contact altogether, we are communicating different messages.

4. How we use our eyes plays a very important role in our everyday communication and in our relationships.

D The following sentences contain information from the reading "Facial Communication." The sentences are in jumbled order. Number the sentences *1–7* to show the correct order for a paragraph about the reading.

____ **a.** We are also, however, capable of putting expressions on our face that deceive people and don't allow them to perceive what we are really feeling.

____ **b.** Common facial expressions, such as happiness or fear, easily express how we feel and are fairly easy to interpret.

____ **c.** By putting a sad expression on your face, for example, you can actually start to feel sad.

____ **d.** Our facial expressions can express how we feel, hide how we feel, and even affect how we feel.

____ **e.** Finally, according to the facial feedback hypothesis, it seems that simply adopting a certain facial expression can influence our emotional state.

____ **f.** However, research shows that women are usually better than men at reading facial expressions.

____ **g.** For example, if we are feeling sad, but don't want other people to know, we can mask our sadness with a happy expression.

E Look at the sentences in Activity D. Decide which three sentences have too much detail to go into a summary of the reading "Facial Communication." Write out the remaining four sentences to produce a well-written summary of the text.

F Go back to the opening sentence that you chose to begin a summary of the reading "Eye Communication" in Activity C. Write three more sentences to complete a summary of the most important information in that reading.

Chapter 6
Touch, Space, and Culture

1 Thinking about the topic ⓡ ⓥ

Work with a partner and brainstorm a list of as many different situations as you can in which it is permissible, or acceptable, for one person to touch another person in your culture. Note which part of the body is used to make the touch, on which part of the body the touch may occur, and who the toucher and the touched might be.

Example:

> A stranger might tap (touch lightly with his or her fingers) another stranger on the shoulder in order to get that person's attention.

The following verbs that describe different ways of touching may help give you some ideas.

caress	kiss	smack
hug	pat	nudge
poke	slap	tickle

2 Skimming ⓡ

> You can get a general idea of a text before you read it just by skimming, which is reading subheadings and the first couple of lines of each paragraph.

Skim through the text. Look at the subheadings and read no more than the first two lines of each paragraph. As you read, answer the following questions:

Paragraph 1 What is a technical term for touch communication?

Paragraph 2 Who usually touches whom when the meaning of the touch is to communicate positive emotions?

Paragraph 3 Can "playful" touching sometimes be aggressive?

Paragraph 4 What are three things that a controlling touch may influence?

Paragraph 5 When does ritualistic touching typically occur?

Paragraph 6 What is an example of a "task-related" touch?

Paragraph 9 Who avoids touching people of the opposite sex more: younger or older people?

Reading 1

THE MEANINGS OF TOUCH

Tactile communication, or communication by touch, also referred to as **haptics**, is perhaps the most primitive form of communication. Developmentally, touch is probably the first sense to be used; even in the womb the child is stimulated by touch. Soon after birth, the child
5 is caressed, patted, and stroked. In turn, the child explores its world through touch. In a very short time, the child learns to communicate a wide variety of meanings through touch. Not surprisingly, touch also varies with your relationship stage. In the early stages of a relationship, you touch little; in intermediate stages (involvement and intimacy),
10 you touch a great deal; and at stable or deteriorating stages, you again touch little.

Touch may communicate five major meanings.

Positive emotions

Touch may communicate positive emotions mainly between intimates
15 or others who have a relatively close relationship. Among the most important of these positive emotions are support, appreciation, inclusion, sexual interest or intent,
20 and affection.

Playfulness

Touch often communicates our intention to play, either affectionately or aggressively. When touch is used in this manner, the playfulness
25 de-emphasizes the emotion and tells the other person that it is not to be taken seriously. Playful touches serve to lighten an interaction.

Control

Touch also may control the behaviors, attitudes, or feelings of the other person. Such control may communicate various messages. To ask for compliance, for example, we touch the other person to
30 communicate "Move over," "Hurry," "Stay here," and "Do it." Touching to control may also communicate status and dominance. The higher-status and dominant person, for example, initiates touch. In fact, it would be a breach of etiquette for the lower-status person to touch the person of higher status.

Ritual

35 Ritualistic touching centers on greetings and departures. Shaking hands to say "hello" or "good-bye" is perhaps the clearest example of ritualistic touching, but we might also hug, kiss, or put our arm around another's shoulder.

Task-relatedness

Task-related touching is associated with the performance
40 of a function such as removing a speck of dust from another person's face, helping someone out of a car, or checking someone's forehead for a fever. Task-related touching seems generally to be regarded positively. In studies on the subject, for example, book borrowers had a more positive
45 attitude toward the library and librarian when touched lightly, and customers gave larger tips when lightly touched by the waitress. Similarly, diners who were touched on the shoulder or hand when given their change in a restaurant tipped more than diners who were not touched.

50 As you can imagine, touching also can get you into trouble. For example, touching that is too positive (or too intimate) too early in a relationship may send the wrong signals. Similarly, playing too roughly or holding someone's arm to control their movements may be resented. Using ritualistic touching incorrectly or in ways
55 that may be culturally insensitive may likewise get you into difficulty.

Touch avoidance

As much as we have a need and desire to touch and to be touched by others, we also have a tendency to avoid touch from certain people or in certain circumstances. Among the important findings is that touch avoidance is positively related to communication apprehension,
60 or fear or anxiety about communicating: People who fear oral communication also score high on touch avoidance. Touch avoidance also is high among those who self-disclose little; touch and self-disclosure are intimate forms of communication, and people who are reluctant to get close to another person by self-disclosure also seem
65 reluctant to get close through touch.

Older people have higher touch avoidance scores for opposite-sex persons than do younger people. Apparently, as we get older, we are touched less by members of the opposite sex and this decreased frequency of touching may lead us to avoid touching. Males score
70 higher than females on same-sex touch avoidance. This accords well with our stereotypes. Men avoid touching other men, but women may and do touch other women. Women, it is found, have higher touch avoidance scores for opposite-sex touching than do men.

1 Reading for details ®

A Match each category of touch to one of the five situations described.

   a. Positive Emotions

   b. Playfulness

   c. Control

   d. Ritual

   e. Task-relatedness

   ___ **1.** A teacher holds a student's arm and leads her down the hall to see the principal.

   ___ **2.** A husband and wife walk arm in arm down the street.

   ___ **3.** Two college students give each other a high five when they meet on campus.

   ___ **4.** A child tickles his friend during recess on the playground.

   ___ **5.** As a sales assistant gives you your change, your two hands touch for a split second.

B According to the section of the text on Touch Avoidance, decide if the correct completion of the sentences below is the phrase *more than* or *less than.* Circle your choice.

   1. People who fear communicating touch people *more than / less than* people who do not fear communication situations.

   2. People who don't mind revealing things about themselves touch others *more than / less than* people who don't like to disclose personal information.

   3. Older people touch people of the opposite sex *more than / less than* younger people.

   4. Men avoid touching men *more than / less than* women avoid touching women.

   5. Women avoid touching men *more than / less than* men avoid touching women.

2 The passive voice Ⓦ ®

Passive sentences are found frequently in academic discourse, so it is important to be able to recognize the passive and use it correctly.

There is, of course, a big difference in meaning between an active and a passive sentence. Compare, for example:

   X touches Y.   X is touched by Y.

In the first sentence, the verb is active. X, the subject, is the one who touches Y and Y receives X's touch. In the second sentence, X is still the grammatical subject, but the verb is passive. It is Y who touches X and X who receives Y's touch.

A According to the information in the text, decide if the active or passive form of the verb *touch* correctly completes the following sentences.

1. A newborn baby _____ its mother soon after birth.
   a. touches   b. is touched by

2. When a relationship deteriorates, people _____ each other less.
   a. touch   b. are touched by

3. In order to control someone's behavior or attitudes, sometimes a person _____ another person.
   a. touches   b. is touched by

4. It is not as acceptable for a higher-status person to _____ a lower-status person as it is for the opposite to happen.
   a. touch   b. be touched by

5. Research shows that customers tend to give larger tips if they _____ their server lightly.
   a. touch   b. are touched by

6. Research also shows that if a librarian _____ you while handing you a book, you are more likely to have a positive opinion of the librarian.
   a. touches   b. is touched by

7. We tend to _____ people less if we like them less.
   a. touch   b. be touched by

B Think back to your brainstorm when doing the Thinking About the Topic task on page 137. Write a short paragraph about situations in your culture when it is permissible to touch or to be touched by another person. Use both active and passive verbs in your sentences.

3 Word families Ⓥ

> You can expand your vocabulary when learning new words by simultaneously learning other words that belong to the same word family as the new words.

A The words in the left column appear in the text. Find the noun forms of these words, which also appear in the text.

1. avoid (v)   _____

2. disclose (v)   _____

3. dominant (adj)   _____

4. greet (v)   _____

5. intimate (adj)   _____

6. playful (adj)   _____

7. ritualistic (adj) _____

8. tip (v)   _____

9. vary (v)   _____

B Use either the noun form or the non-noun form of the words in Activity A to complete the short text.

The amount of touching _____ depending on the degree of

_____ between two people. Although in certain _____

situations, such as during a _____ , people who are not so

_____ may touch by shaking hands. Research shows that certain

people who don't like to _____ personal details about themselves

try to _____ touching other people as much as possible. Touch

_____ also may occur as people get older.

4 Summarizing Ⓦ

Look back at the guidelines on writing summaries on page 135. Write a one-sentence summary of the section of the text on task-related touching and a one-sentence summary of the section on touch avoidance.

1 Gathering data Ⓡ Ⓦ

> Doing some small-scale research and gathering data relating to the topic that you are going to read about helps provide a context for your reading.

A Before reading this text, spend five minutes outside the classroom with a partner and secretly observe two people talking. Notice the following details:

Space: How far apart are the two people from each other?

Touch: Do they ever touch? Where? For how long?

Gestures: How do they use their hands and heads? How do they position their bodies?

Eye contact: How much do they look at each other? Is one person making more eye contact than the other?

Facial expressions: What facial expressions do you observe?

B Report back to the class on what you observed and what relationship you think the two people have. Explain your reasoning. Also, if possible, describe what you think they may have been talking about.

2 Predicting Ⓡ

> According to this text, people create different amounts of distance between themselves depending on their relationships. The four different distances named in the text are:
>
> **a.** intimate distance   **c.** social distance
> **b.** personal distance   **d.** public distance

Which picture do you think represents people at each of these different distances?

Reading 2

SPATIAL MESSAGES

Space is an especially important factor in interpersonal communication, although we seldom think about it. Edward T. Hall, who pioneered the study of spatial communication, called this area **proxemics**. We can examine this broad area by looking at proxemic distances.

5   Four proxemic distances correspond closely to the major types of relationships. They are intimate, personal, social, and public distances.

Intimate distance

In intimate distance, ranging from the close phase of actual touching to the far phase of 6 to 18 inches, the presence of the other individual is unmistakable. Each individual experiences the sound, smell, and
10   feel of the other's breath. The close phase is used for lovemaking and wrestling, for comforting and protecting. In the close phase, the muscles and the skin communicate, while actual words play a minor role. The far phase allows people to touch each other by extending their hands. The individuals are so close
15   that this distance is not considered proper for strangers in public. Because of the feeling of inappropriateness and discomfort (at least for some Americans), the eyes seldom meet but remain fixed on some remote object.

Personal distance

We carry a protective bubble defining our personal distance,
20   which allows us to stay protected and untouched by others. Personal distance ranges from 18 inches to about 4 feet. In the close phase, people can still hold or grasp each other, but only by extending their arms. We can then take into our protective bubble certain individuals – for example, loved
25   ones. In the far phase, you can touch another person only if you both extend your arms. This far phase is the extent to which you can physically get your hands on things; hence, it defines in one sense the limits of your physical control over others. At times, we may detect breath odor, but generally at
30   this distance etiquette demands that we direct our breath to some neutral corner so as not to offend.

In a crowded elevator, you are forced to be at an intimate distance with people who are strangers. To maintain their personal space, therefore, people usually avoid eye contact.

Social distance

At the social distance, ranging from 4 to 12 feet, you lose the visual detail you had in the personal distance. The close phase is the distance at which you conduct impersonal business or interact at a social
35   gathering. The far phase is the distance at which you stand when someone says, "Stand away so I can look at you." At this distance,

business transactions have a more formal tone than when conducted in the close phase. In offices of high-ranking officials, the desk and the visitor's chair are often positioned so that clients are kept at least
40 this distance away. Unlike the intimate distance, where eye contact is awkward, the far phase of the social distance makes eye contact essential – otherwise, communication is lost. The voice is generally louder than normal at this level. The distance enables you to avoid constant interaction with those with whom you work without seeming rude.

Public distance

45 Public distance ranges from 12 to no more than 25 feet. In the close phase, a person seems protected by space. At this distance, you're able to take defensive action should you feel threatened. On a public bus or train, for example, you might keep at least this distance from a drunk. Although you lose the fine details of the face and eyes, you're still close
50 enough to see what is happening.

At the far phase, you see others not as separate individuals but as part of the whole setting. People automatically establish a space of approximately 30 feet around important public figures and they seem to do this whether or not there are guards preventing their coming
55 closer. This far phase is the distance by which actors on stage are separated from their audience; consequently, their actions and voices have to be somewhat exaggerated.

The specific distance that you'll maintain between yourself and any given person depends on a wide variety of factors. Among the most
60 significant are gender (women sit and stand closer to each other than do men in same-sex dyads, and people approach women more closely than they approach men), age (people maintain closer distances with similarly aged others than they do with those much older or much younger), and personality (introverts and highly anxious people
65 maintain greater distances than do extroverts). Not surprisingly, you'll maintain shorter distances with people you're familiar with than with strangers, and with people you like than with those you don't like.

1 Making a chart Ⓐ Ⓦ

When information in a text contains categories with contrasting characteristics, it is often possible to create a chart to display that information. If you can find a way to do this in your note-taking, it is always a good idea because information displayed in this way is easy to review later for a test.

Look at the grid one student has created from the information in this text. Some of the details have been entered into the grid. Review the text and complete the grid with the missing details.

	Distance in close phase	Distance in far phase	Typical relationship between people	Examples of what one can see or smell	Amount of eye contact or voice level used
Intimate distance			lovers		
Personal distance	18 inches			breath odor	
Social distance		12 feet			more eye contact, louder voice
Public distance			dangerous-looking strangers, public figures		

2 Using adverbs Ⓦ

Often, sentences start with the subject of the verb followed by the verb. Adverbs or adverbial phrases, which can have many different functions, can also start a sentence. When the adverb comes at the beginning of the sentence, the writer is drawing attention to the adverb or adverbial phrase. Usually, adverbial phrases at the beginning of sentences are followed by a comma. (See the bottom of the page for some examples of adverbs and adverbial phrases.)

Because this is a reading about the importance of where people are in relation to each other and space, it is not surprising that adverbial phrases describing location are the focus of many sentences.

A Find the following in the reading:

1. one example of an adverbial phrase of location at the beginning of a sentence in the section "Intimate Distance"

2. two examples of adverbial phrases of location at the beginning of a sentence in the section "Personal Distance"

3. three examples of adverbial phrases of location at the beginning of a sentence in the section "Social Distance"

4. four examples of adverbial phrases of location at the beginning of a sentence in the section "Public Distance"

B Write two sentences using adverbial phrases of location at the beginning of the sentences to describe the following:

1. the close phase of intimate distance and the far phase of intimate distance

2. the close phase of social distance and the far phase of social distance

3. eye contact in the close phase of intimate distance and eye contact in the social distance

C Notice the adverbial phrase "not surprisingly" at the beginning of a sentence in the last paragraph of the reading. When this type of adverb is at the beginning of a sentence, it gives the writer's attitude or feeling toward the information in the whole of the sentence that follows.

Circle the adverbs below that tell the author's feelings when they come at the beginning of a sentence:

evidently	approximately	in this case	in other countries
clearly	finally	unexpectedly	at the moment
at first	apparently	on Sundays	fortunately

3 Answering a short-answer test question

On a short-answer quiz, it is not unusual for your instructor to ask you to contrast two things or concepts. When you write the answer, make sure you clearly separate the two items being contrasted by using transitional expressions of contrast, such as the following:

on the other hand   in contrast   however

A Answer the following test questions on the reading "Spatial Messages." Use your chart in Task 1, adverbs of location from Task 2, and the transitional expressions of contrast in your answers. Remember, too, that a good answer to a short-answer test question should include examples.

1. Describe the difference between intimate distance and social distance.

2. Describe the difference between the close phase of public distance and the far phase.

B Share your answers with a partner and critique each other's answers. What score would you give each other out of a maximum 10 points, and why?

4 Exploring key concepts

In this text, you have read about the distances people normally keep between each other in different situations. What happens when you do not follow these norms? Try this experiment to find out and also to deepen your understanding of the concepts in the text.

A Stand next to another student in the class. Talk to each other about any topic. (Choose something neutral, such as what you did or are planning to do over the weekend.) After a couple of minutes, stop. Do not move at all. Notice how close to each other you are standing. This distance should feel comfortable to both of you. Does it?

B Take one half-step toward the other person and continue talking for another few minutes. Stop and discuss with your partner how you each felt talking at this distance.

C Both of you take one step back. Continue talking for a few more minutes. Stop and discuss how the extra distance affected your feelings and the way in which you used your voice and eyes.

D Try the same experiment again. This time, choose someone of a different culture or gender. Describe any differences you feel at different distances with this person.

E Write about the experiment. In your writing, use transitional expressions of contrast and adverbial phrases of location to describe your different distances and feelings.

1 Skimming ®

Skim the reading "Nonverbal Communication and Culture." Circle the topics that are covered in the reading.

- Gender differences in touch behavior
- Cultural differences in spatial behavior
- Cultural differences in eye contact
- Gender differences in gestures
- Cultural differences in touch behavior
- Differences across cultures in male facial expressions

2 Thinking about the topic ®

Discuss the following questions in small groups or with the whole class.

1. What gestures would be considered offensive in your culture that you think might not be considered offensive in other cultures?
2. Are there situations in your culture when people should not smile? Explain.
3. In Chapter 5, Reading 3, "Eye Communication," you read about eye contact. Does your culture have eye contact rules that you think are different from other cultures' that you have read about or know about? Explain.
4. When people greet each other in your culture, what do they do? Does the behavior vary depending on whether the people are young, old, male, female, friends, strangers, and so on? Explain.

Reading 3

NONVERBAL COMMUNICATION AND CULTURE

Throughout this unit, we've seen a few cultural and gender differences in nonverbal communication. Cultural variations in certain channels of communication, however, have become the focus of sustained research. Here, we consider just a sampling of the relationship between
5 culture and nonverbal communication expressed through gestures, facial expressions, eye communication, and touch.

Culture and gesture

There is much variation in gestures and their meanings among different cultures. Consider a few common gestures, such as the ones below, that you may use often without thinking, but that could easily
10 get you into trouble if you used them in another culture.

Hand gestures may mean very different things in different cultures.

- Folding your arms over your chest would be considered defiant and disrespectful in Fiji.
- Waving your hand would be rude in Nigeria and Greece.
- Gesturing with your thumb would be rude in Australia.
15 - Tapping your two index fingers together would be considered an invitation to sleep together in Egypt.
- Pointing with your index finger would be impolite in many Middle Eastern countries.
- Bowing to a lesser degree than your host would be considered a
20 statement of your superiority in Japan.
- Inserting your thumb between your index and middle finger in a clenched fist would be viewed as a wish that evil would befall a person in some African countries.
- Resting your feet on a table or a chair would be insulting and
25 disrespectful in some Middle Eastern countries.

Culture and facial expression

The wide variations in facial communication that we observe in different cultures seems to reflect which reactions are publicly permissible rather than a fundamental difference in the way emotions are facially expressed. For example, it is considered "forward," or inappropriate, for Japanese women to reveal broad smiles; therefore, many Japanese women will hide their smiles, sometimes with their hands. Women in the United States, on the other hand, have no such restrictions and so are more likely to smile openly. Thus, the difference may not be in the way different cultures express emotions but rather in the societies' display rules, or rules about the appropriate display of emotions in public. The well-documented finding that women smile more than men, for example, is likely due, in part, to display rules that allow women to smile more than men.

Culture and eye communication

Not surprisingly, eye messages vary with both culture and gender. For example, Americans consider direct eye contact an expression of honesty and forthrightness, but the Japanese often view this as showing a lack of respect. A Japanese person will glance at the other person's face rarely, and then only for very short periods. Therefore, interpreting another's eye contact messages according to one's own cultural rules is a risky undertaking; eye movements that you may interpret as insulting may have been intended to show respect.

Women make eye contact more and maintain it longer (both in speaking and in listening) than men. This holds true whether women are interacting with other women or with men. This difference in eye behavior may result from women's great tendency to display emotions. When women interact with other women, they display affiliative and supportive eye contact, whereas when men interact with other men, they avert their gazes.

Cultural differences also exist in the ways people decode the meaning of facial expressions. For example, American and Japanese students judged the meaning of a smiling and a neutral facial expression. The Americans rated the smiling face as more attractive, more intelligent, and more sociable than the neutral face. In contrast, the Japanese rated the smiling face as more sociable, but not as attractive – and they rated the neutral face as more intelligent.

Culture and touch

The several functions and examples of touching discussed earlier in this chapter were based on studies in North America; in other cultures, these functions are not served in the same way. In some cultures, for example, some task-related touching is viewed negatively and is to be avoided. Among Koreans, it is considered disrespectful for a store owner to touch a customer when, say, handing back change; it is considered too intimate a gesture. A member of another culture, however, who is used to touching may consider the Korean's behavior cold and aloof. Muslim children are socialized not to touch children of the opposite sex; consequently, their behavior can easily be interpreted as unfriendly by American children who are used to touching one another.

Some cultures – including many in southern Europe and the Middle East – are contact cultures; others are noncontact cultures, such as those of northern Europe and Japan. Members of contact cultures maintain close distances, touch one another in conversation, face each other more directly, and maintain longer and more focused eye contact. Members of noncontact cultures maintain greater distances in their interactions, touch each other rarely (if at all), avoid facing each other directly, and maintain much less direct eye contact. As a result of these differences, problems may occur. For example, northern Europeans and Japanese may be perceived as cold, distant, and uninvolved by southern Europeans – who may in turn be perceived as pushy, aggressive, and inappropriately intimate.

Greetings Around the World

Something that we do every day is really quite complex. We greet people. It's not something that we usually think about very much, but the nonverbal behavior that we use to greet people depends on a lot of different factors. How well do we know the person? When did we last see the person? Was it yesterday or two months ago? Is the person male or female? Older or younger? Higher status or lower status? A friend, a relative, or an acquaintance? And where is the other person from?

Some possible greetings in the United States are a handshake, a single light kiss on the cheek, a hug, a wave, a light slap on the back, or a simple nod and a smile. In some countries, such as France, you kiss lightly on two cheeks. In others, such as Holland and Serbia, three kisses are the rule. In Japan and South Korea, a bow is often required. In Thailand and Cambodia, you put the palms of your hands together in front of you in a praying motion. There are cultures where the handshake should be strong and firm and others where the handshake should be light and soft. And there are still others where fingers just touch quickly and softly.

What do you do? Shake hands? Kiss? Bow? Hug? Or do you rub noses like the Eskimos? It's really not so simple, is it?

1 The passive voice Ⓦ Ⓡ

Very often in academic writing, the doer of an action (sometimes called the agent) is not known or important. The focus is on *what* is done, rather than *who* did it. In such cases, the passive voice may be used and the agent not mentioned at all in the sentence. In this paragraph, for example, you have seen the following sentence structures: *the agent is not known*; *the passive voice may be used*; *the agent is not mentioned.*

A Find examples of the passive in this text by doing the following:

1. Look at the bulleted list in the Culture and Gesture section of this text. Find four examples of the passive and circle them.

2. Find two examples of the passive in the section Cultural and Facial Expression and circle them.

3. Circle all examples of the passive in the section Culture and Touch.

4. The boxed text "Greetings Around the World" is not an academic text. How many examples of the passive can you find in that text?

5. In how many of the examples of the passive that you circled was the agent – the doer of the main verb – mentioned?

B Make sentences about nonverbal behavior in your culture. You can use language such as the following to help you make your sentences.

Doing X would be/might be/is considered to be Y.

Doing X is viewed negatively.

People are socialized to . . .

People who do X in my culture are perceived to be Y.

2 Generalizations about groups of people Ⓦ Ⓡ

One common way to make a generalization about groups of people is to use a plural noun with no article.

~~The~~ men	~~The~~ women	~~The~~ children
~~The~~ Americans	~~The~~ Italians	~~The~~ Russians

However, when the nationality word ends in *-ese*, *-ish*, *-ch*, or *-iss*, you must use the article to generalize about that nationality.

The Chinese   The British   The French

If you use adjective + *people/men/women* and so on, do not use an article:

Chinese people   British men   French women   Mexican children

Skim through the text and then make generalizations about the following groups and the topic given.

1. Nigerians, Greeks, and hand waving
2. Middle Easterners and putting feet on a table or chair
3. men, women, and smiling
4. Japanese women, American women, and smiling
5. women, men, and eye contact
6. the Japanese, Americans, and eye contact
7. Koreans and touching
8. Middle Easterners, northern Europeans, and touching
9. Muslim children, American children, and touching
10. French people, Dutch people, and greeting

3 Transitional expressions

> Writers use transitional expressions to help readers see the relationship between different parts of their text. Like signposts on the road, they show you where you are going and where you have come from. They can show that you are about to read an example, a contrast, a consequence, and so on. Being aware of them can help you to improve comprehension of a text. Using them in your own writing can make your ideas clearer.

Not surprisingly, in this text, which is about differences in body language between cultures and possible misunderstandings because of those differences, we see a large number of transitional expressions of the following types:

Transitional expressions of example: *for example*
Transitional expressions of contrast: *however*
Transitional expressions of result or consequence: *so*

A Look at this analysis of Paragraph 3. Find the transitional expressions in the text that are used to prepare the reader for the underlined words below.

Generalization about when smiling is permissible + <u>Example</u> of a belief in country A + <u>Result</u> of that belief in country A + <u>Contrast</u> with belief in country B + <u>Result</u> of that belief in country B.

B Analyze parts of Paragraphs 4, 6, 7, and 8 in the same way. Find and circle the transitional expressions in the text. Mark them *E* for example, *C* for contrast, and *R* for result.

C Draw from the information in the reading and your discussions of cross-cultural differences in the activities before and after reading the text and write sentences of your own. Follow this sequence:

- Write a generalization.
- Give an example that illustrates that generalization.
- Write about a cultural or gender difference from your first example.
- Write about what may happen as a result of this difference.

4 Collocations

Try to notice when the same adjective occurs frequently with the same noun. These are adjective + noun collocations. The more collocations you know, the easier reading can become because you will anticipate certain phrases before you even read them.

A Without looking back at the reading, make adjective + noun collocations by matching the adjectives on the left with the nouns that they collocate with in the reading. Write the matching adjective on the line to make the collocation.

1. broad _____ eye contact

2. clenched _____ period

3. common _____ finding

4. direct _____ gesture

5. fundamental _____ expression

6. neutral _____ undertaking

7. risky _____ fist

8. short _____ difference

9. well-documented _____ variation

10. wide _____ smile

B With a partner, check the answers by looking for the collocations in the reading. Use each collocation in a new context by making sentences that relate to body language.

5 Synthesizing Ⓐ Ⓡ Ⓦ

> *Synthesizing* means gathering separate ideas and information from different places and putting them together in one place to see if common elements exist. If you know you are going to read about a topic and you have already done some reading on the topic, go back and review those readings. Make a chart that synthesizes the information.

A Reread the opening paragraph of "Nonverbal Communication and Culture." As indicated in the introductory paragraph, you have already read about some instances of cultural and gender differences in nonverbal communication.

B Skim through the six readings in the unit that you have already read and fill in the chart below. Make notes in the chart about any examples of cultural or gender differences from those readings.

	Gender Differences	Cultural Differences
Gestures		
Face		
Eyes		
Touch		
Space		

Chapter 6 Academic Vocabulary Review

The following are some of the words that appear in Chapter 6. They all come from the Academic Word List, a list of words that researchers have discovered occur frequently in many different types of academic texts. If you can learn these words, it should help you when you have a reading in almost any academic discipline. For a complete list of all the Academic Word List words in this chapter and in all the other readings in this book, see the Appendix on pages 213–214.

Reading 1 The Meanings of Touch	Reading 2 Spatial Messages	Reading 3 Nonverbal Communication and Culture
circumstances	automatically	appropriate (adj)
culturally	correspond	display
emphasize	detect	fundamental
initiate	enable	restrictions
reluctant	gender	reveal
similarly	visual	sustain

Complete the following sentences with words from the lists above.

1. It was impossible to _____ her feelings from her facial expression.

2. Unfortunately, in such _____ there is nothing that can be done.

3. It is very difficult to _____ a conversation with him because he gives very little nonverbal feedback.

4. It may be necessary to place _____ on what he can and cannot say.

5. We need someone to _____ this project so that we can get started.

6. Take this note. It will _____ you to get into the meeting.

7. How you look at people and how close to them you stand may _____ your feelings toward them.

8. Sometimes we use gestures to _____ a point that we are trying to make.

9. One _____ difference between northern and southern Europeans is the amount of information they communicate through their body language.

10. A gesture in one country may have a meaning that does not _____ to the same meaning in another country.

11. We often judge people by _____ appearances, not their words and actions.

12. Workers are often _____ to disagree with their managers.

Practicing Academic Writing

In Unit 3, you have learned about the different elements of body language and how the way we use body language sends out messages. You will use this information to write a short handbook.

Nonverbal Communication in My Culture

Produce a handbook that will help someone who is not a member of your culture understand how your culture uses body language. Divide the handbook into sections. Each section will describe one of the following elements of nonverbal communication: gestures, facial expressions, eye communication, touch, and space. In each section, you will summarize what you have learned about that element of body language. You will tell the visitor to your culture what different elements of body language mean. You will also explain what body language to expect and what to avoid.

PREPARING TO WRITE

Outlining

When you have to write a document that has different sections, it is best to do careful planning. You need to decide what headings and subheadings you might use and what is to go under each heading. The best way to do this is to create an outline.

Outlining before writing an essay can be very simple; you can just create a skeleton outline of your main ideas. However, when writing a report or handbook with different sections, it is best to do quite a bit of planning. You can start with a skeleton outline, but then you should expand it to include more specific examples and details.

Many students develop their own system of numbers and letters when they create outlines, but there is one principle that is used by most people: indentation. The more specific your idea, the more it is indented to the right underneath the more general idea to which it belongs.

```
I. xxxxxxxxxxxxxxxxxxxxxxxxxxxx
   A. xxxxxxxxxxxxxxxxxxxx
         1. xxxxxxxxxxxxxxx
         2. xxxxxxxxxxxxxxx
   B. xxxxxxxxxxxxxxxxxxx
         1. xxxxxxxxxxxxxx
         2. xxxxxxxxxxxxxx
II. xxxxxxxxxxxxxxxxxxxxxxxxxxxxx
   A. xxxxxxxxxxxxxxxxxxxx
```

A Decide what the main sections of your handbook will be and create a skeleton outline.

B Decide how you are going to organize each section of your handbook into logical subsections with clear subheadings. This will make it easier for you to write and easier for your reader to follow. Make sure that your subheading language is parallel; that is, that each subheading uses the same type of grammar and language.

Work with a partner and discuss which of the following subsections and subheadings for the topic of Gestures will lead to a clear and well-organized section of your handbook.

1.

Emblem gestures

Regulator gestures

Gestures foreigners should avoid

2.

Gestures for visitors to know

Gestures for visitors to use

Gestures for visitors to avoid

3.

The gesture for "Everything is fine"

The gesture for "He's crazy"

The gesture for "I need money"

4.

Rude gestures

Finger and hand gestures

Head gestures

C Analyze the structure of the readings in this unit. Notice how many have subheadings and what those subheadings are. Also notice whether the reading starts immediately with a subheading or if there is an introduction to the reading.

D Decide what subsections you want to use and expand the skeleton outline that you have created so far into a more detailed outline.

E Parts of your handbook will contain information that is specific to your culture. It is therefore unlikely that you will be able to use information from this unit to help you write those parts. However, you will also need to have general statements about each body language type. Here, the readings can help you.

F Go back through each reading in this unit and see if there are parts of the reading that you would like to summarize or paraphrase. Look back at the sections on paraphrasing on page 80 and on summarizing on page 135. Then write your paraphrases and summaries, following the guidelines and making sure that you do not plagiarize.

G Use some of the pre-writing strategies that you have learned so far (Making a List on page 51 and Freewriting on page 105). Use those techniques to start getting down on paper some ideas and phrases that you can use in each section of your handbook.

Writing a handbook or a report

A handbook or a report is not the same as an essay, and so it does not have the same organization and parts. However, in some respects, each section of your report is a mini-essay. Each section probably stills need an introductory section that makes some general remarks about the content of the section and that explains how you have organized the section and what the reader can expect to read about.

Since each section of your handbook is like a mini-essay, it is advisable to write and revise one section of the handbook first so that you have fully worked out how each section will be structured. Once you have done that, it will be easier to work on the remaining sections.

A Look at your detailed outline. Choose one section of your handbook and start writing it. Use any notes that you made during the Preparing to Write section to help you. Include any summaries or paraphrases that you have already written.

B Revise this section to make sure that you are satisfied with the subsections you have created and the general structure of the section.

C Now write the other sections of your handbook. Use the type of subheadings that you created in your first section and its structure to guide you.

D Remember that your first draft does not have to be perfect. A first draft is just a beginning point. It provides you with some text that you can change until you are satisfied with the final product.

Section Titles

Make sure you know the rules for capitalizing the titles of your headings and subheadings. The basic rules are:

- Always capitalize the first letter of the first and last words.
- All nouns, verbs, adjectives, adverbs, and pronouns should start with a capital letter.
- Articles and prepositions should start with a lowercase letter. (Some style guides suggest that any preposition of five letters or more should be capitalized.)

A Have a friend read through your handbook. If the friend is from the same or a similar culture to yours, ask him or her to confirm that what you have written about body language in your culture is accurate. Ask your friend also to look for parts of your handbook that are unclear or confusing. Use your friend's feedback to help you revise.

B Look again at those parts of your handbook that contain summaries or paraphrases of parts of the readings in the unit. Make sure that you have followed the guidelines for writing summaries and paraphrases properly and that you have not plagiarized.

C When you produce a report or a handbook on a computer and the report has different sections and subsections, you can make the headings stand out according to how important they are. This will help your reader follow your report more easily. You can use the following to make headings stand out in different ways:

- Use a large typeface size
- Use all uppercase letters
- Use bold

D If your report is being written on a computer and you are connected to the Web, you can also make your report visually appealing by downloading a few photos and adding them to your handbook. If you don't know how to do this, ask someone in the class. Usually someone can teach you these skills.

E Read through your essay to edit it.

1. In your handbook, you probably make several generalizations. Look back at Task 2, Generalizations About Groups of People, on page 154 and see that you have used articles correctly.

2. Remember that generalizations often require hedging language. Is what you have written true for *everyone* in your culture or just for *most*, *many*, or *some* people? Do people *always* use the body language you mention or *usually*, *often*, or *generally*? Go back and see if your generalizations require hedging language.

3. Transitional expressions will help your reader follow your writing (see Task 3, Transitional Expressions, on page 155). Go back through your handbook and see if you need to add some transitional expressions of example, contrast, comparison, or result.

4. Have you tried to use the passive voice in your handbook? Check places where the passive voice is required and see if you have used it correctly.

5. Read through your essay now for possible spelling mistakes, punctuation errors, subject-verb agreement errors, and incorrect use of past tense and articles. Make corrections whenever you find errors.

Unit 4
Interpersonal Relationships

In this unit, you will study two important kinds of relationships that develop during your life. In Chapter 7, you will think about what defines a friend and how relationships develop, including how to break the ice during a first encounter. You will also read about how the Internet is playing an increasing role in relationships in many people's lives. In Chapter 8, you will read about love. You will examine the question of why we are attracted to some people, but not to others, and you will learn that there are many different types of love and ways of loving.

Contents

In Unit 4, you will listen to and speak about the following topics.

Chapter 7 Friendship	Chapter 8 Love
Reading 1 What Is Friendship?	**Reading 1** Attraction Theory
Reading 2 The First Encounter	**Reading 2** Types of Love
Reading 3 The Internet and Relationships	**Reading 3** Gender Differences in Loving

Skills

In Unit 4, you will practice the following skills.

R Reading Skills	**W** Writing Skills
Thinking about the topic Predicting Personalizing the topic Previewing art Skimming Reading for details Increasing reading speed Comprehension after speed reading Reading for main ideas Thinking critically	Efficient sentence structure Understanding paragraph structure Journal writing Summarizing Paraphrasing Using quotations The passive voice
V Vocabulary Skills	**A** Academic Success Skills
Using new words in context Collocations Prepositions Words related to the topic *Similar* and *different*	Outlining practice Exploring key concepts Mnemonics Preparing for a test Taking notes

Learning Outcomes

Write an essay in which you analyze one or two of your personal relationships.

Previewing the Unit

> Before reading a unit (or chapter) of a textbook, it is a good idea to preview the contents page and think about the topics that will be covered. This will give you an overview of how the unit is organized and what it is going to be about.

Read the contents page for Unit 4 on page 164 and do the following activities.

Chapter 7: Friendship

A In the second reading in Chapter 7, we focus on how you should behave the first time you meet someone whom you would like to get to know better. Imagine you are meeting someone for the first time. Decide which of the following topics would be good to talk about (check *Yes),* and which would not (check *No).* When you finish, decide which topic would be the best choice, and which the worst. Give reasons.

	Yes	No
1. A neutral topic like the weather or the traffic	☐	☐
2. A controversial topic like politics or religion	☐	☐
3. A personal problem that you have	☐	☐
4. A personal problem that the other person has	☐	☐
5. Something the other person is wearing or carrying	☐	☐

B In the final section of this chapter, you will read about how people meet and maintain friendships on the Internet. Talk about how you use social media, such as Facebook or MySpace, to stay in touch with your friends. Answer these questions in a group.

1. Do you belong to a social networking group like Facebook or MySpace? If you do, how often do you use these sites and what do you do on them?

2. How important is the Internet in maintaining your friendships? Do you have some friendships that are mostly maintained online, not face-to-face?

3. Do you think the quality of an online friendship is different from a face-to-face friendship? In what ways? Which type of friendship is stronger?

Chapter 8: Love

A How would you define the difference between love and friendship?

B Read these two proverbs. Discuss which one you think is more often true, and why.

Birds of a feather flock together. (In other words, we are usually more attracted to people who are similar to ourselves.)

Opposites attract. (In other words, we are usually more attracted to people who are different from ourselves.)

Chapter 7
Friendship

1 Thinking about the topic ®

Discuss the following questions with a partner.

1. How would you define "a friend"?
2. Make a list of the different activities that you have done with friends in the past week.
3. How many close friends do you have? Do you have close friends of the opposite sex?

2 Predicting ®

In this text, we learn that we may become friends with people because of five different values that they may bring to our lives. The five values are listed on the left; definitions for these five values are listed in the box on the right.

a. a utility value

b. an affirmation value

c. an ego support value

d. a stimulation value

e. a security value

utility: usefulness
affirmation: showing and confirming what is true and good
ego: sense of one's own importance
stimulation: providing a source of interest
security: a sense of being safe

A The following examples are given in the text to illustrate the five different friendship values. Before reading the text, try to match each example to one of the values of friendship, a–e, above. Write the letter in the blank.

____ **1.** A friend may enable us to expand our worldview and come into contact with issues and concepts of previously unfamiliar cultures and ideas.

____ **2.** A friend may help us to recognize our leadership abilities, our athletic prowess, or our sense of humor.

____ **3.** A friend does nothing to hurt us or to emphasize or call attention to our inadequacies or weaknesses.

____ **4.** A friend may attract us because he or she is particularly bright and might assist us in getting better grades, in solving our personal problems, or in getting a better job.

____ **5.** A friend may enable us to more easily view ourselves as worthy and competent individuals.

B Compare your answers with a partner's.

Reading 1

WHAT IS FRIENDSHIP?

Friendship has engaged the attention and imagination of poets, novelists, and artists of all kinds. On television, friendships have become almost as important as romantic pairings. And friendship also interests a range of interpersonal-communication researchers.
5 Throughout your life you'll meet many people, but out of this wide array you'll develop few relationships you would call friendships. Yet, despite the low number of friendships you may form, their importance is great.

Definition and characteristics

Friendship is an *interpersonal relationship* between two interdependent
10 persons that is *mutually productive* and characterized by *mutual positive regard*. First, friendship is an interpersonal relationship; communication interactions must have taken place between the people. Further, the relationship involves a "personalistic focus"; friends react to each other as unique, genuine, and irreplaceable individuals. Second, friendships must
15 be mutually productive. They must not be destructive to either person. Third, friendships are characterized by mutual positive regard. Liking people is essential if we are to call them friends.

In North America, friendships clearly are a matter of choice; you choose – within limits – whom your friends will be. And most researchers
20 define friendship as a voluntary relationship, a relationship of choice. The density of U.S. cities and the ease of communication and relocation make many friendships voluntary. But throughout human history, in many parts of the world – for example, in small villages – relationships

friendship
an interpersonal relationship characterized by mutual positive regard

traditionally have not been voluntary. In these settings, you simply form
relationships with those in your village. You don't have the luxury of
selecting certain people to interact with and others to ignore. You must
interact with and form friendships and romantic relationships with
members of the community simply because these are the only people
you come into contact with on a regular basis. This situation is changing
rapidly however, as Internet use becomes nearly universal. With access
to people from all over the world via the Internet, more and more
relationships will become voluntary.

Friendship needs

For still another answer to the question of
what a real friendship is, consider the needs
that friends serve. For example, if you need
to be the center of attention or to be popular,
you might select friends who allow you or
encourage you to be the center of attention, or
who tell you that you're popular. One way to
analyze the needs that friendships serve is to
consider the values or rewards that you seek to
gain through your friendships.

Friends may serve a stimulation function. For example, they may teach them how to eat noodles with chopsticks.

Utility: Someone who may have special
talents, skills, or resources that will prove
useful to you in achieving your specific goals
and needs. For example, you might become friends with someone
who is particularly bright, because such a person might assist you in
getting better grades, in solving problems, or in getting a better job.

Affirmation: Someone who will affirm your personal value and
help you to recognize your attributes. For example, you might develop
a friendship with someone because of that person's appreciation
of your leadership abilities, your athletic prowess, or your sense of
humor.

Ego Support: Someone who behaves in a supportive, encouraging,
and helpful manner. For example, you might seek friendships that
would help you view yourself as worthy and competent.

Stimulation: Someone who introduces you to new ideas and new
ways of seeing the world and helps you to expand your worldview. For
example, you might form friendships with those who bring you into
contact with previously unfamiliar people, issues, religions, cultures,
and experiences.

Security: Someone who does nothing to hurt you or to emphasize
or call attention to your inadequacies or weaknesses. For example, you
might select friends because you wouldn't have to worry about them
betraying you or making negative comments about you.

As your needs change, the qualities you look for in friendships also change. In many instances, old friends are dropped from your close circle to be replaced by new friends who better serve these new needs.

Friendship stages

Friendships develop over time in stages. At one end of the friendship
70 are strangers, or two persons who have just met, and at the other end are intimate friends. Of course, over time, many relationships also come to an end, or dissolve.

Contact: The first stage of friendship is initial contact of some kind. At the contact stage, the interaction often is characterized
75 by awkwardness. Because the other person is not well known to you, you're more guarded rather than open and expressive, and supportiveness, positiveness, and equality are all difficult to manifest in any meaningful sense.

Involvement: In the involvement period, the other person
80 becomes a casual friend – someone we would go to the movies with, sit with in the cafeteria or in class, or ride home from school with. You begin to communicate with confidence, express yourself openly, and develop a genuinely positive attitude toward the other person. A clear sense of "we-ness," or togetherness, emerges.

85 **Close and Intimate Friendship:** At this stage, you and your friend see yourselves more as an exclusive unit. Your uncertainty about each other has been significantly reduced, you are able to predict each other's behavior with considerable accuracy, and there is greater positivity, supportiveness, and openness. You become more other-oriented
90 and more willing to make significant sacrifices for this friend and the friend does the same. Each person in an intimate friendship is truly equal.

Dissolution: Let's begin by dispelling one great myth and that is that relationship dissolution is always bad. It isn't necessarily. Often, relationships deserve to be dissolved. For example, friendships may become destructive or overly competitive – as can occur in a variety of work situations – and may be better put aside. If a "friend" makes your self-disclosures public or otherwise betrays your confidence, and if this becomes a pattern that is repeated over and over again, it may be time to move from the level of friendship to that of seldom-seen acquaintanceship.

Ten Things We Do with Friends

A number of online surveys ask people what they do with their friends. Here are ten of the most frequent answers.

1. Go shopping at the mall
2. Eat out at a nice restaurant
3. Go to the movies
4. Stay home and watch a show on TV
5. Play a game (video game, board game, cards)
6. Take a trip
7. Train for a race
8. Go to a dance club or comedy club
9. Just hang out together
10. Go out to a special event together: concert, sports event, etc.

---

1 Using new words in context Ⓥ Ⓡ

> After learning new words and phrases, try to use them soon afterwards in a personal context.

A Look at these sentences from the reading and the boxed text. Use the context to try to guess the approximate meaning of the words and phrases in bold.

1. Throughout your life you'll meet many people, but out of this **wide array** you'll develop few relationships you would call friendships. (Lines 5–6)

2. Third, friendships are characterized by **mutual positive regard**. Liking people is essential if we are to call them friends. (Lines 16–17)

3. And most researchers define friendship as a **voluntary** relationship . . . (Lines 19–20)

4. With access to people from all over the world **via** the Internet, more and more relationships will become voluntary. (Lines 30–32)

5. For example, you might develop a friendship with someone because of that person's appreciation of your leadership abilities, your athletic **prowess** . . . (Lines 50–53)

6. At the contact stage, the interaction often is characterized by awkwardness. Because the other person is not well known to you, you're more **guarded** rather than open . . . (Lines 74–76)

7. Let's begin by **dispelling** one great myth and that is that relationship dissolution is always bad. It isn't necessarily. Often, relationships deserve to be dissolved. (Lines 95–97)

8. Just **hang out** together. (Boxed text)

B Work with a partner and answer the following questions. Try to use the words and phrases in bold in your answers.

1. Do you or someone you know collect things? What **wide array** of things do you or the person you know have in the collection?

2. Name a person you know with whom you have a **mutual positive regard**.

3. What sort of things have you done on a **voluntary** basis that other people perhaps have had to be forced to do?

4. Whom do you communicate with **via** e-mail?

5. What special **prowess** do you have now or did you have when you were younger?

6. In what circumstances do you tend to be **guarded**?

7. If you could **dispel** one myth about people from your culture, what would it be?

8. Where do you like to go to just **hang out** with friends?

2 Outlining practice Ⓐ Ⓦ

> Creating an outline of a text gives you a clear idea of its structure and can help you to prepare for a test later.

A Complete the following skeleton outline of "What Is Friendship?"

    I. *Three main characteristics of friendship*

       A. _____

       B. *Mutually productive: no destructiveness*

       C. _____

    II. *Friendship needs*

       A. *Utility: Friend can be useful to you in some way*

       B. _____

       C. _____

       D. _____

       E. *Security: You feel safe with friend*

    III. *Stages*

       A. _____

       B. _____

       C. *Close and intimate: truly equal and more other-oriented*

       D. _____

B Compare your outline with a partner's.

3 Efficient sentence structure Ⓦ

> Sometimes a writer uses a list of words or phrases in a sentence as an efficient way to "pack" a lot of information into one sentence. When writing such lists, commas are usually necessary to separate each item in the list.

A Look at Sentence 3 in Paragraph 2 again:

> . . . friends react to each other as unique, genuine, and irreplaceable individuals.

This means that friends *react to each other as* unique individuals, they *react to each other as* genuine individuals, and they *react to each other as* irreplaceable individuals. However, the writer has been very efficient by using the introductory verb phrase only once, together with the three adjectives.

B Work with a partner and do the following.

1. Find an example of a sentence in Paragraph 5 that lists three nouns. Circle them. Find another sentence in the same paragraph that lists three verb phrases. Circle them.

2. Find a sentence in Paragraph 6 that lists three noun phrases. Circle them.

3. Find a sentence in Paragraph 7 that lists three adjectives. Circle them.

4. Find a sentence in Paragraph 8 that lists five noun phrases. Circle them.

5. Find three more examples of sentences with at least three items in the section Friendship Stages. Circle the listed items.

6. Look again at each of the sentences where you circled. Look at how the words and phrases that you circled connect back to an earlier phrase connected to the stem in the sentence. Underline the earlier phrase.

7. When a writer adds a list of words and phrases to an earlier phrase in a sentence, it is important that each item in the list adds something new. Go back and look at the circled words one more time. Discuss with your partner what new information is added by each word or phrase in the list.

4 Understanding paragraph structure Ⓦ Ⓡ

A Look at the structure of Paragraph 2, which is given here in skeleton form, and then answer the questions.

> _____ (Sentence 1) _____ . First, _____ (Sentence 2) _____ . Further, _____ (Sentence 3) _____ . Second, _____ (Sentence 4) _____ . _____ (Sentence 5) _____ . Third, _____ (Sentence 6) _____ . _____ (Sentence 7) _____ .

1. How many parts are there to the definition of _friendship_ in Sentence 1?

2. What are the functions of Sentences 2 and 3, Sentences 4 and 5, and Sentences 6 and 7?

3. Which words signal that the writer is moving from one part of the definition to another?

4. What does the word _further_ signal?

5. What are the functions of Sentences 3, 5, and 7?

B Look at the third section, Friendship Stages, and construct a paragraph similar to the model above. Think about which signal words you might use since you will be creating a paragraph about change over time.

C Look at the boxed text "Ten Things We Do with Friends." Construct a paragraph that has a structure similar to that of Paragraph 2. To do this, you will need to find a way to sort the things we do with friends into three groups.

5 Journal writing ⓦ

You can use the topic of a reading to write about personal matters in a journal. Writing regularly in a second language in a journal can help you to become more used to using the language. Remember, your journal is private; you don't have to show it to anyone.

Write a journal entry on one of the following topics.

1. What having a friend and being a friend means to me
2. The end of a friendship – how it broke up, and why
3. The different friends in my life and the different functions they serve

1 Personalizing the topic ⓡ

Discuss the following questions with a partner or in a small group.

   1. Why do you think you have trouble or do not have trouble making new friends when you enter a new environment?

   2. Where are some good places to go to meet new people?

   3. If you were to give advice to someone who is not from your culture on what to do to make contact with and become friends with someone from your culture, what advice would you give?

2 Previewing art ⓡ

Before reading a text, it is a good idea to examine any photographs and illustrations that accompany it. Reading the captions for the art can be helpful, too.

Look at the picture in the text and discuss the following questions with a partner.

   1. Where are these people?

   2. How well do you think they know each other? How can you tell?

   3. How interested is the woman on the left in talking to the woman on the right? How can you tell from her body language?

   4. How interested is the woman on the right in talking to the woman on the left? How can you tell from her body language?

3 Skimming ⓡ

A Skim though the text "The First Encounter." Look at the subheadings. Notice the numbered lists. Just read the first sentence of each item, which may be very short. Take one minute to do this.

B Work with a partner. Tell each other what you think the main idea of this text is going to be. Tell each other any details that you remember from your skim of the reading.

Reading 2

THE FIRST ENCOUNTER

The first stage in a friendship is initial contact. However, many people have trouble meeting people and making new friends, so here are a few suggestions for how to act during the first encounter. Although they are divided into the "nonverbal encounter" and the "verbal
5 encounter," recognize that these must be integrated for any effective encounter to occur.

The nonverbal encounter

nonverbal communication concerns every aspect of you that sends messages to another person. On the basis of these messages, the other person forms an impression of you – an impression that will be
10 quickly and firmly established.

1. Establish eye contact. Eye contact is the first nonverbal signal to send. The eyes communicate an awareness of, and interest in, the other person.

2. While maintaining eye contact, smile and further signal your
15 interest in this other person.

3. Concentrate your focus. The rest of the room should be nonverbally shut off from your awareness. Be careful, however, that you do not focus so directly as to make the person uncomfortable.

4. Establish physical closeness, or at least lessen the physical distance
20 between the two of you. Approach, but not to the point of discomfort; your interest in making contact is obvious.

5. Throughout this nonverbal encounter, maintain a posture that communicates an openness, a willingness to enter into interaction with the other person. Hands crossed over the chest or clutched
25 around your stomach are exactly the kind of postures that you want to avoid. These are often interpreted as signalling an unwillingness to let others enter your space.

6. Respond visibly. Assuming that your nonverbal communication is returned, respond to it visibly with another smile or a head nod.

30 7. Reinforce positive behaviors. Reinforce those behaviors of the other person that signal interest and a willingness to make contact. Reinforce these by responding positively to them; again, nod or smile, or somehow indicate your favorable reaction.

8. Avoid overexposure. Nonverbal communication works to make
35 contact or to signal interest, but it can cause problems if it is excessive or if it is not followed by more direct communication. Consequently, if you intend to make verbal contact, do so after a relatively short time.

nonverbal communication
messages communicated by your eyes, face, and body, as well as by your clothes and other possessions that you display

The verbal encounter

1. Introduce yourself. Try to avoid trite and clichéd opening lines; it is probably best to simply say, "Hi, my name is Pat."

2. Focus the conversation on the other person. Get the other person involved in talking about him- or herself. No one enjoys talking about anything more. Also, it will provide you with an opportunity to learn something about the person you want to get to know.

3. Compliment the other person; be sincere, but complimentary and positive. If you cannot find anything to compliment the person about, then it is probably wise to reassess your interest in this person.

4. Be energetic. No one likes a lethargic, slow-moving, non-dynamic partner. Demonstrate your high energy level by responding facially with appropriate affect, smiling, talking in a varied manner, being flexible with your body posture and gestures, asking questions as appropriate, and otherwise demonstrating that you are really there.

5. Stress the positives. In the discussion of interpersonal effectiveness, it was noted that positiveness was one of the major qualities of effectiveness. It also contributes to a positive first impression simply because we like and are attracted to a positive person more than to a negative one.

6. Avoid negative and too intimate self-disclosures. Enter a relationship gradually and gracefully. Disclosures should come in small degrees and along with reciprocal disclosures. Anything too intimate or too negative early in the relationship will create a negative image. If you cannot resist self-disclosing, then try to stick to the positives and to those matters that would not be considered overly intimate.

7. Establish commonalities. Seek to discover in your interaction those things you have in common with the other person – attitudes, interests, personal qualities, third parties, places, and so on.

8. Avoid *Yes/No* questions, *Yes/No* answers, and rapid-fire questions. Ask questions that are open-ended, questions that the receiver may answer at some length. Similarly, respond with answers more complete than simply "yes" or "no." Be careful, too, that your questions do not appear to be an interrogation.

1 Reading for details Ⓡ

A The reading "The First Encounter" offers suggestions for how to act during a first encounter with a stranger. State whether the author recommends (write *R*) or does not recommend (write *NR)* the following behaviors.

____ **1.** Keep your arms crossed over your chest.

____ **2.** Get as close to the other person as possible.

____ **3.** Focus your attention on the other person.

____ **4.** Try not to look into the other person's eyes.

____ **5.** When the other person gives you a positive sign, you should give a positive sign, like a smile, in return.

____ **6.** After you have made contact nonverbally, don't wait too long before you start talking.

____ **7.** Introduce yourself simply by saying, "Hi, my name is . . . "

____ **8.** Try to keep the conversation mostly about yourself, so the other person can learn as much about you as possible.

____ **9.** If possible, give a compliment. For example, say, "I really like your shoes."

____**10.** Quickly start talking about your very deepest feelings.

____**11.** Talk about people, places, and leisure activities that you both know about.

____**12.** Ask many questions that begin, "Are you," "Do you," "Have you," and so on.

B Compare your answers with a partner's.

2 Exploring key concepts Ⓐ

> You can sometimes deepen your understanding of concepts in a reading by doing a role play that makes use of what you have newly learned.

Work in groups of three. One student will be an observer. The other two students will act out the following situation:

Two students are seated next to each other, waiting for their professor to come into class. They do not know each other. One of the students wants to get to know the other student and initiates a conversation.

After the conversation, the observer will report on how well the initiator used nonverbal and verbal strategies in engaging the other student in a first-encounter conversation.

3 Summarizing Ⓦ Ⓡ

> Summarizing a reading not only helps you deepen your understanding of new subject matter but also prepares you if you have to include new information in a writing assignment.

A Using information from the text, write a summary of one of the following topics.

1. Nonverbal and verbal behaviors you should use when you first meet someone whom you would like to get to know

2. Nonverbal and verbal behaviors you should avoid when you first meet someone whom you would like to get to know

B Work with a student who wrote about the opposite topic from you. Read his or her summary and decide how effective it is as a summary. Are the main points clearly expressed? Is there too much detail? Help your partner improve his or her summary, according to the guidelines on page 135.

1 Words related to the topic ⓥ

A Many of the words in Reading 3 relate to the Internet. Work with a partner and define the words and phrases below, which are taken from this reading. Also, talk about any personal connections you may have with the concepts that these words represent.

1. social networks

2. online dating

3. e-mail

4. chat rooms

5. the Web

6. a (Web) site

7. virtual (relationship)

B In this reading, there are some comparisons made between the world of the Internet and the "real" world. Which of the following words from the reading do you think will be contrasted with the words in the list in Activity A? Write the number of the word from Activity A in the blank.

____ **1.** School, work, and church settings

____ **2.** Snail mail

____ **3.** Face-to-face

____ **4.** Personal ads in newspapers

2 Predicting ⓡ

In this reading, research about the impact of the Internet on interpersonal relationships is summarized. Discuss whether you think this sentence from the reading will contain a positive or a negative verb. Why?

> . . . "research to date generally *does not paint/paints* a positive picture of the Internet's impact on people's connections with one another."

3 Increasing reading speed ⓡ

Use this text as an opportunity to practice your speed-reading skills. Before you start, review the guidelines for faster reading on page 34 in Chapter 2.

Read the text "The Internet and Relationships" to practice reading for speed. Time yourself. When you finish, turn to the tasks that begin on page 183 and write down how long it took you to read the text.

Reading 3

THE INTERNET AND RELATIONSHIPS

To meet prospective friends and romantic partners, people used to be limited to school, work, and religious organizations. Then came the "club scene," personal ads in newspapers, and video dating services. More recently, the Internet has dramatically expanded opportunities
5 for people to meet and develop relationships through social networks, online dating services, e-mail, chat rooms, and news groups.

Critics see these trends as leading to the death of face-to-face interactions, widespread loneliness and alienation, and millions being lured into dangerous liaisons by unscrupulous people. But
10 research to date generally paints a positive picture of the Internet's impact on people's connections with one another. For example, the Web offers a wealth of opportunities to interact for those normally separated because of geography, physical infirmity, or social anxiety. Internet groups also offer support and information for those with
15 grave illnesses (e.g., cancer, multiple sclerosis, diabetes, or AIDS). Of course, the anonymous nature of Internet communication *does* make it easy for dishonest individuals to take advantage
20 of others, so it's smart to be cautious about revealing personal information online.

In a short period of time, the Internet has become an
25 indispensable vehicle for making acquaintances and developing relationships. One survey based on a nationally representative sample of
30 American adults reported that 31 percent (representing 63 million people) knew someone who had used a dating Web site, and 11 percent (representing 22 million adults) had visited such a site to meet people. Among those who used online dating sites, a majority
35 (52%) reported "mostly positive" experiences, although a sizeable number (29%) had "mostly negative" experiences.

Although critics are concerned that Internet relationships are superficial, research suggests that virtual relationships are just as intimate as face-to-face ones and are sometimes even closer. Further,
40 many virtual relationships migrate to face-to-face interactions. When people do decide to move beyond an Internet-based relationship, they typically first exchange letters via "snail mail" or talk on the telephone.

Actual meetings usually take place only after telephone contact. Researchers find that romantic relationships that begin on the Internet seem to be just as stable over two years as traditional relationships. This same study reported that 22 percent of the participants said that they were living with, had become engaged to, or were married to someone they had first met on the Internet.

The Internet has also assumed tremendous importance in maintaining established relationships. In a poll of 1,000 Internet users, 94 percent reported that the Internet made it easier for them to communicate with friends and family who live far away, and 87 percent said that they use it regularly for that purpose. Although some social critics have predicted that Internet use will reduce face-to-face interactions, in fact, Internet users typically maintain their social involvements while cutting back on TV time.

The differences between Internet and face-to-face communication require psychologists to reexamine the established theories and principles of relationship development. For example, good looks and close physical proximity are powerful factors in initial attraction in the real world. On the Internet, where people form relationships sight unseen, these factors are irrelevant. Online, similarity of interests and values kicks in earlier and assumes more power than it does in face-to-face relationships. One study found that pairs of strangers who chatted on the Internet liked each other more than if they had talked face-to-face. But in another study of pairs randomly assigned to either face-to-face or Internet chat conversations, the face-to-face group felt more satisfied with the experience and felt a higher degree of closeness and self-disclosure with their partners.

Self-disclosure is another relationship issue affected by the differences in the two types of communication. Because the Internet is shrouded in the cloak of anonymity, people take great risks in self-disclosure. Thus, feelings of intimacy can develop more quickly. Sometimes this experience can provide a false sense of intimacy, which can create uncomfortable feelings if a face-to-face meeting ensues – that is, meeting with a stranger who knows "too much" about you. Of course, face-to-face meetings can also go smoothly.

Additional research in this fascinating area will not only provide valuable information about virtual relationships but will reveal interesting new perspectives on face-to-face relationships.

1 Comprehension after speed reading ®

A Write the time it took you to read the text in minutes or fractions of a minute on Line a (e.g., 7.2 minutes). Divide the number of words by the number of minutes and write the answer on Line c. This is your words-per-minute reading speed for this reading.

a. time to read in minutes   _____

b. number of words   ___690___

c. wpm (b/a)   _____

d. number correct   _____

e. percent correct (dx10)   _____

B Now test your understanding by answering these multiple-choice comprehension questions without looking back at the text. Choose the best answer from the choices listed. Have your teacher check your answers and then fill in Lines d and e above. When reading at speed, a good goal is to get 70 percent of your answers correct. If you get 100 percent correct, you are probably reading too carefully.

1. A good alternative title for this text would be ___ .

    a. The Benefits of Internet Relationships

    b. The Dangers of Internet Relationships

    c. Superficiality and Internet Relationships

2. Historically, ___ came first as a way for people to meet prospective romantic partners.

    a. personal ads in newspapers

    b. the "club scene"

    c. the work setting

3. In a survey of Americans, approximately ___ said that they knew someone who had used an online dating service.

    a. one-quarter

    b. one-third

    c. one-half

4. In a survey of Americans who had used an online dating service, approximately ___ said that they had had a positive experience.

    a. one-quarter

    b. one-third

    c. one-half

5. In a study of Americans who met face-to-face after meeting online, approximately ___ went on to live with that person.

    a. one-quarter

    b. one-third

    c. one-half

6. Research has shown that online relationships are ___ face-to-face relationships.

    a. never as intimate as

    b. sometimes more intimate than

    c. always equally as intimate as

7. Psychologists are surprised that people form close relationships online because ___ has always played a key role in relationship development.

    a. physical proximity

    b. going out to places together

    c. sharing similar interests

8. Research has shown that Internet users have ___ face-to-face involvement with others compared to those who don't use the Internet much.

    a. significantly less

    b. significantly more

    c. about the same amount of

9. Because there is more anonymity in an online relationship, people tend to be ___ .

    a. more prepared to reveal intimate things about themselves

    b. dishonest about themselves

    c. reluctant to tell other people about themselves

10. Revealing intimate things about yourself online before meeting someone in person is ___ .

    a. never a good thing to do

    b. always a good thing to do

    c. sometimes a bad thing to do

2 Collocations Ⓥ

> Some words combine frequently with other words that belong to different parts of speech. For example, the noun *role* can collocate with a verb (*play*), an adjective (*major*), and a preposition (*in*). This means that you should notice and learn collocational combinations of words such as "to play a major role in."

A Look at these collocations from the reading. From the list of words below these collocations, find the word from the reading that is missing to form a collocational combination. Then find two other words in the list that could go in the blank to form other frequent collocational combinations. Some of the words below may be used more than once.

1. to paint a/an _____ picture

2. to _____ a wealth of opportunities

3. to be shrouded in _____

4. to _____ a false sense of _____

5. to assume _____ importance

6. to cut back on _____

7. to take _____ risks

a cloak	offer
assistance	one's own importance
attractive	positive
create	provide
disturbing	secrecy
feel	security
great	spending
have	support
help	tremendous
huge	TV time
intimacy	undue
major	work
mystery	

B How many adjectives can you find in the reading that collocate with the word *relationships*? What are they?

_____ relationships

3 Paraphrasing W R

Practice your paraphrasing skills from time to time; they can help you improve your overall language ability. In addition, if you paraphrase something on a topic that your instructor might include in an assignment, you will have something ready to use.

A Work in groups of three students. Each student paraphrases a different excerpt from the reading, below. Before starting, look again at the guidelines about how to paraphrase on page 80.

1. "Critics see these trends as leading to the death of face-to-face interactions, widespread loneliness and alienation, and millions being lured into dangerous liaisons by unscrupulous people."

2. "For example, good looks and close physical proximity are powerful factors in initial attraction in the real world. On the Internet, where people form relationships sight unseen, these factors are irrelevant."

3. "Because the Internet is shrouded in the cloak of anonymity, people take great risks in self-disclosure. Thus, feelings of intimacy can develop more quickly. Sometimes this experience can provide a false sense of intimacy, which can create uncomfortable feelings if a face-to-face meeting ensues."

B Critique the paraphrases in your group. Check to see that the sentence structure has been rearranged and different vocabulary has been used, but that the essential meaning of the excerpts remains the same.

4 Exploring key concepts A W

A Write three or four questions to ask your classmates about their use of the Internet for relationships. Find out about such things as how they:

- meet new friends
- stay in touch with friends
- tell people about themselves

B Make a sheet to record your classmates' answers. Walk around the room, asking your questions of every student and recording their answers.

C Do some simple math on the answers and then report your findings to the class:

About half the class . . .
Nobody in the class . . . , and so on

Chapter 7 Academic Vocabulary Review

The following are some of the words that appear in Chapter 7. They all come from the Academic Word List, a list of words that researchers have discovered occur frequently in many different types of academic texts. If you can learn these words, it should help you when you have a reading in almost any academic discipline. For a complete list of all the Academic Word List words in this chapter and in all the other readings in this book, see the Appendix on pages 213–214.

Reading 1 What Is Friendship?	Reading 2 The First Encounter	Reading 3 The Internet and Relationships
access	aspect	assigned
assist	concentrate	irrelevant
despite	contribute	migrate
expand	flexible	prospective
via	reassess	trends
voluntary	visibly	widespread

Complete the following sentences with words from the lists above.

1. Be _____ . Find a time to meet your friend that is good for him even if it inconveniences you a little bit.
2. Throughout the country, there was a _____ feeling that the economy was about to collapse.
3. After this recent experience, I am going to have to _____ my feelings about the value of social media in making new friends.
4. I'm traveling to Warsaw _____ Berlin. I'll be stopping there for a few days.
5. _____ the fact that we are so different, we are still best friends.
6. In the experiment, she _____ people to groups depending on their experience with using social media.
7. It is very difficult to _____ with so much happening all around us.
8. She liked him a lot, but she did not see him as a _____ husband.
9. My decision to sign the papers was _____ .
10. There is one _____ of their relationship that I just don't understand.
11. Joining a club can help you _____ your circle of friends.
12. Mayumi felt that what anyone else thought of her friendship with David was _____ .

Developing Writing Skills

In this section, you will learn about and practice including quotations in your writing. At the end of the unit, you will be given your unit writing assignment, in which you will be asked to use information from the readings in the unit. When you include this information in your assignment, you will include quotations.

Using Quotations

In the Developing Writing Skills sections on pages 80 and 135, you have learned how to paraphrase and how to summarize. In each case, you have learned how to avoid plagiarizing by using your own words to include information and ideas from another writer.

A third way to include another writer's information and ideas is to use quotations, that is, the actual words that the writer used. You may want to do this because the writer has expressed the information and ideas well and the words perfectly support what you are trying to say. Also, using the writer's actual words will show your instructor that you have read and understood a reading very thoroughly and thought critically about it.

When you use quotations in your writing, you must follow certain conventions. These conventions often depend on which academic field you are writing in or how your instructor tells you to include quotations. Minimally, the conventions include:

- Using the author's name
- Referring to the source that the writer's words came from: book, article, Web site, etc.
- Putting quotation marks around the author's actual words
- Not changing any words from the originals inside the quotation marks

Reading 1 in Chapter 7 is from the following source material. (A complete list of the source material for all readings is on page 215.)

The Interpersonal Communication Book, by Joseph A. DeVito

A Look at this excerpt from a student's writing and see how she included quotations from Reading 1 in her essay. Then answer the questions that follow. As you answer the questions, try to work out rules for using quotations in your writing.

In *The Interpersonal Communication Book*, Joseph DeVito writes, "One way to analyze the needs that friendships serve is to consider the values or rewards that you seek to gain through your friendships." For example, DeVito says that some friends provide a stimulation value. According to DeVito, this means that you might develop a friendship with someone because this person could "bring you into contact with previously unfamiliar people, issues, religions, cultures, and experiences." One of my closest friends, for example, is from . . .

1. What font style does the student use for the title of the book?
2. How often does the student refer to the title of the book each time she quotes from it?
3. When does the student use the author's full name and when does she use only his last name?
4. Find all the uses of capital letters in this piece of writing and explain them.
5. Find all the examples of commas used in this piece of writing and explain them.
6. Make a rule for the placement of punctuation at the beginning and end of a quotation.

B Reading 3 in Chapter 7 comes from the following source:

Psychology Applied to Modern Life: Adjustment in the 21st Century,
by Wayne Weiten, Margaret A. Lloyd, Dana S. Dunn, & Elizabeth Yost Hammer
(Note that when there are more than two authors, you only need to give the first author's last name and add "et al.," which means "and others.")

Look at how another student included quotations from Reading 3. In this case, the student has made several mistakes in her use of quotations. First, compare the student's writing to the original text in Paragraph 2 on page 181. Then, find the errors and circle them. Finally, work with another student to compare answers and work out how to correct the mistakes.

Some people find it very difficult to make friends or meet people. Perhaps they are shy or they live in a small town where there are not many opportunities to make friends. For such people, the Internet is ideal. As Weiten et al write, "the Web offers many opportunities to interact for those normally separated because of geography, physical infirmity, or social anxiety." Of course, as they also point out the anonymous nature of Internet communication does "make it easy for dishonest individuals to take advantage of others".

C Reading 2 in Chapter 7 is also from *The Interpersonal Communication Book* by Joseph A. DeVito. Write a short paragraph on what to say to someone during a first encounter. Include the following three quotations from page 177 to support the advice:

"No one enjoys talking about anything more."
"Compliment the other person; be sincere, but complimentary and positive."
"Establish commonalities."

Chapter 8
Love

Personalizing the topic ®

> Thinking about your personal connections to a topic before you read about it will help you absorb new information on that topic.

A Ask and answer the following questions with a partner. Use the structures that follow each question to help you frame your answer.

1. Which people in public life, for example, movie stars, singers, athletes, and TV personalities, do you find attractive?

> I find _____ very attractive.

2. What sort of men or women are you attracted to? Give as much detail as possible, for example, eye color, type of hair, height, nationality, intelligence, values, and so on.

> I am (very) attracted to men/women who _____ .
> I find men/women who _____ (very) attractive.

3. What sort of men or women do you find unattractive? Give details as above.

> I am not (at all) attracted to men/women who _____ .
> I don't find men/women who _____ (very) attractive.

B According to this text we are often attracted to people who "look, act, and think" like ourselves. Consider your descriptions of people that you find attractive. Discuss with your partner to what extent these descriptions could also be descriptions of yourself.

C In the boxed text "Murdoch and Deng," you will read about a couple who are married to each other and who are very different from each other. Talk with your partner about people you know who are married to each other and who are very different. Talk about the ways in which they are different.

Reading 1

ATTRACTION THEORY

Attraction theory holds that people form relationships on the basis of attraction. You are no doubt drawn, or attracted, to some people and not to others. In a similar way, some people are attracted to you and some are not. If you're like most people, then your attraction to others may be based on one or more of five major factors: similarity, proximity, reinforcement, physical attractiveness and personality, and socioeconomic and educational status.

Similarity

If you could construct your mate, according to the similarity principle, it's likely that your mate would look, act, and think very much like you. Generally, people like those who are similar to them in nationality, race, abilities, physical characteristics, intelligence, and attitudes. Research also finds that you're more likely to help someone who is similar in race, attitude, general appearance, and even first name.

Sometimes people are attracted to their opposites, in a pattern called **complementarity**; for example, a dominant person might be attracted to someone who is more submissive. Generally, however, people prefer those who are similar.

Proximity

If you look around at people you find attractive, you will probably find that they are the people who live or work close to you. People who become friends are the people who have the greatest opportunity to interact with each other. Proximity, or physical closeness, is most important in the early stages of interaction – for example, during the first days of school (in class or in dormitories). The importance of proximity as a factor in attraction decreases, though always remains significant, as the opportunity to interact with more distant others increases.

Reinforcement

Not surprisingly, you're attracted to people who give rewards or reinforcements, which can range from a simple compliment to an expensive cruise. You're also attracted to people you reward. That is, you come to like people for whom you do favors; for example, you've probably increased your liking for a person after buying them an expensive present or going out of your way to do them a special favor. In these situations, you justify your behavior by believing that the person was worth your efforts; otherwise, you'd have to admit to spending effort on people who don't deserve it.

People are most often attracted to people who are similar to them in many ways.

complementarity
the concept that people are attracted to those who are different from themselves

Physical attractiveness and personality

It's easily appreciated that people like physically attractive people more than they like physically unattractive people. What isn't so obvious is that we also feel a greater sense of familiarity with more-attractive people than with less-attractive people; that is, we're more likely to think we've met a person before if that person is attractive. Additionally, you probably tend to like people who have a pleasant rather than an unpleasant personality (although people will differ on what is and what is not an attractive personality).

Socioeconomic and educational status

Popular belief holds that among heterosexual men and women, men are more interested in a woman's physical attributes than in her socioeconomic status. And indeed, research shows that women flirt on the Internet by stressing their physical attributes, whereas men stress their socioeconomic status. Interestingly, there is evidence that men too consider a woman's socioeconomic status when making a romantic relationship decision – but whereas women find higher socioeconomic status more attractive, men find just the opposite. Men report greater likelihood of a romantic relationship with a woman lower in socioeconomic status than they are. Further, men find women with a higher educational level (which is often responsible for the higher socioeconomic status) less likeable and less faithful and, as a result, see less likelihood of a romantic relationship with such women.

Murdoch and Deng

Similarity may be the most common reason that people find each other attractive; however, there are plenty of counter examples. Usually, the counter example involves a beautiful, young, not-so-well-off woman and an older and/or not-so-attractive, extremely wealthy, powerful man.

Take Rupert Murdoch, for example. In 1999, Rupert Murdoch, a 68-year-old Australian, married Wendi Deng, a stunningly beautiful, 30-year-old Chinese-born woman. Murdoch at the time was (and still is) a billionaire and one of the most powerful men in the world. Deng at the time had a middle income job and was the daughter of a Chinese factory worker.

More than 10 years later, the two are still married and they have two children.

1 Reading for main ideas Ⓡ

The main ideas in this text are the five factors that are said to play a role in whether one finds someone attractive or not. State these main ideas by completing the five sentences below.

Similarity
One is very likely to find someone attractive if _____

_____

Proximity
People that you find attractive are likely to _____

_____

Reinforcement
We often find attractive people who _____

_____

Physical Attractiveness and Personality
People like people more when they are _____

_____

Socioeconomic and Educational Status
Men are usually attracted to _____

but women _____

2 Mnemonics Ⓐ

It is very likely that in a test of the material covered in this reading, an instructor might ask the following question:

> According to attraction theory, what are the five factors that play a role in determining whether one person is attracted to another?

A One way to remember the five factors is to create a mnemonic. A mnemonic is a memory aid. The following mnemonic is an abbreviation. Interpret this mnemonic:

> 2S 2P R

B Another way to make a mnemonic is to make a word. Interpret this word:

> SuPPeRS

C You can also make a mnemonic by creating a sentence that will remind you of the items you are trying to remember. Your sentence should be something that creates an unusual or funny image in your head. Interpret this sentence:

> Papa says porcupines sometimes run.

D Make a mnemonic of your own for the factors in attraction theory. Make up either an abbreviation, a word, or a sentence.

3 Preparing for a test Ⓐ Ⓡ Ⓦ

Remember, a complete answer on a test involves not only knowing the meaning of a term, but also being able to provide an example of it.

A For the five factors in attraction theory, fill out a chart similar to the one below.

Factor	Meaning	Example
1.		
2.		
3.		
4.		
5.		

B Study your chart and remember the mnemonic that you created in Task 2. Turn to page 193 and answer the test question at the beginning of Task 2 without looking back at your notes.

4 Prepositions (V)

> Prepositions can be very challenging when learning English. Some prepositions, however, are always associated with certain content words (nouns, verbs, and adjectives). So, when you learn the content words, learn the prepositions that usually go with them.

A The following content words appear in this reading. Which prepositions did they occur with? Match the prepositions to the words without looking back at the text.

in	of	on	to	with

1. to admit _____
2. to be a factor _____
3. to be based _____
4. to be drawn _____
5. to go out of your way _____
6. to have a familiarity _____
7. to have a greater likelihood _____
8. to have an opportunity _____
9. to interact _____
10. to spend an effort _____

B Make sentences with the phrases above using concepts from the reading.

5 Journal writing (W)

> If you know that your instructor may ask you to write a paper on the topic that you are studying, keep a response journal. Your journal may provide you with ideas for your writing later on. In a response journal, you react to what you read by saying how you feel about the writer's ideas and whether you agree with them. Remember that your journal is for your eyes only, so write whatever you want.

Write a journal entry that responds to the reading "Attraction Theory." Evaluate the five different factors. Write about the factors you agree have played a role in whom you are and are not attracted to.

Words related to the topic Ⓥ

> Remember that the more words you already know relating to a topic, the easier it is to read about that topic.

Read the following words or phrases taken from the text. They all relate in some way to the topic of love. Then read the sentences that follow. For each sentence, find words or phrases that can complete the sentence. Write the corresponding letters in the blanks.

a. mate (n)
b. fidelity
c. obsessive
d. fall in love
e. compatibility
f. erotic
g. passion
h. make a commitment

i. jealous
j. lover
k. possessive
l. establish a relationship
m. intimacy
n. partner
o. desire (n)

1. In a relationship, there are two people – you and your ___, ___, ___ .

2. Three stages in a relationship may be when you ___, ___, and ___ .

3. Strong emotions felt in a relationship are ___ and ___ .

4. In a healthy relationship, people usually want to avoid someone who is ___, ___, or ___ .

5. A(n) ___ -experience is one involving strong physical or sexual feelings.

6. Three qualities people look for in a close, loving relationship are ___ , ___ , and ___ .

Reading 2

TYPES OF LOVE

Love is a feeling characterized by closeness and caring and by intimacy, passion, and commitment. Although there are many theories about love, the conceptualization that captured the attention of interpersonal researchers and continues to receive research support
5 is a model proposing that there is not one but six types of love.

Eros: Beauty and sexuality

Like Narcissus, who fell in love with the beauty of his own image, the erotic lover focuses on beauty and physical attractiveness, sometimes to the exclusion of qualities you might consider more important and more lasting. Also, like Narcissus, the erotic lover has an idealized
10 image of beauty that is unattainable in reality. Consequently, the erotic lover often feels unfulfilled. Not surprisingly, erotic lovers are particularly sensitive to physical imperfections in the ones they love.

Ludus: Entertainment and excitement

Ludus love is experienced as a game. The ludic lover sees love as fun, a game to be played. The better you can play the game, the greater the
15 enjoyment. To the ludic lover, love is not to be taken too seriously; emotions are to be held in check lest they get out of hand and make trouble; passions never rise to the point at which they get out of control. A ludic lover is self-controlled, always aware of the need to manage love rather than allowing it to be in control.

20   Not surprisingly, the ludic lover retains a partner only as long as the partner is interesting and amusing. When interest fades, it's time to change partners. Perhaps because love is a game, sexual fidelity is of little importance. Also, not surprisingly, recent research shows that people who score high on ludic love are more likely to score high on
25 narcissism.

Storge: Peaceful and slow

Storge love (a word that comes from the Greek for "familial love") lacks passion and intensity. Storgic lovers set out not to find lovers but to establish a companionable relationship with someone they know and with whom they can share interests and activities. Storgic love
30 is a gradual process of unfolding thoughts and feelings; the changes seem to come so slowly and so gradually that it is often difficult to define exactly where the relationship is at any point in time. Sex in storgic relationships comes late and, when it comes, it assumes no great importance.

Mania: Elation and depression

35 Mania is characterized by extreme highs and extreme lows. The manic lover loves intensely and at the same time intensely worries about the loss of the love. This fear often prevents the manic lover from deriving as much pleasure as possible from the relationship. With little provocation, the manic lover may become extremely jealous. Manic
40 love is possessive and obsessive; the manic lover must possess the beloved completely. In return, the manic lover wishes to be possessed, to be loved intensely. The manic lover's poor self-image seems capable of being improved only by being loved; self-worth comes from being loved rather than from any sense of inner satisfaction. Because love
45 is so important, danger signs in a relationship are often ignored; the manic lover believes that if there is love, then nothing else matters.

Pragma: Practical and traditional

The pragma lover is practical and seeks a relationship that will work. Pragma lovers want compatibility and a relationship in which their important needs and desires will be satisfied. They're concerned
50 with the social qualifications of a potential mate even more than personal qualities; family and background are extremely important to the pragma lover, who relies not so much on feelings as on logic. The pragma lover views love as a useful relationship that makes the rest of life easier. So the pragma lover asks such questions about a
55 potential mate as "Will this person earn a good living?" "Can this person cook?" "Will this person help me advance in my career?" Not

There are many different types of love and lovers, and the way we love another person may change over time.

surprisingly, pragma lovers' relationships rarely deteriorate. This is partly because pragma lovers have chosen their mates carefully and emphasize similarities. Another reason is that they have realistic
60 romantic expectations.

Agape: Compassionate and selfless

Agape is a compassionate, egoless, self-giving love. The agapic lover loves even people with whom he or she has no close ties. This lover loves the stranger on the road, even though the two
65 of them will probably never meet again. Agape is a spiritual love, offered without concern for personal reward or gain. This lover loves without expecting that the love will be reciprocated. Jesus, Buddha, and Gandhi preached this unqualified
70 love, agape. People who believe in Yuan, a Chinese concept that comes from the Buddhist belief in predestiny, are more likely to favor agapic (and pragmatic) love and less likely to favor erotic love.

75   While combinations of these six types of love are possible, the six major types illustrate the complexity of any love relationship. The six styles should also make it clear that different people want different things, that each person
80 seeks satisfaction in a unique way. The love that may seem lifeless or crazy or boring to you may be ideal for someone else. At the same time, another person may see these very same negative qualities in the love you're seeking.

    Remember, too, that love changes. A relationship that began as
85 pragma may develop into ludus or eros. A relationship that began as erotic may develop into mania or storge.

1 Reading for details Ⓡ Ⓥ

The names given to the five different types of love in this text are technical terms and are not common words in English. Some of them might not be known to native speakers and may not appear in the dictionary. You will be able to understand what they mean only by a careful reading of the text.

Match the sentence opener on the left with its completion on the right to find a description of each type of lover.

___ **1.** The ludic lover

___ **2.** The storgic lover

___ **3.** The pragma lover

___ **4.** The manic lover

___ **5.** The erotic lover

___ **6.** The agapic lover

a. is emotionally intense.

b. seeks a physically beautiful lover and an intensely physical relationship.

c. does not seek a commitment in a relationship, just sex and fun.

d. has a spiritual kind of love for humanity as a whole.

e. is most satisfied with a partner with similar needs and interests and who makes everyday life more comfortable.

f. is emotionally cool and seeks friendship rather than intense passion.

2 Taking notes Ⓐ Ⓦ

When studying a text about a group of related categories, it is a good idea to learn the terms used for these categories and to make a list of the main characteristics of each one.

A Look at these notes showing in list form the main characteristics of ludic love.

Ludic love:
   1. *love is a game – fun*
   2. *emotions kept under control*
   3. *change partners – interest fades*
   4. *sexual fidelity – not impt.*
   5. *Ludic lovers score high on narcissism*

B Make notes for one of the other types of love and then compare your notes with those of a student who took notes on the same type of love as you.

C Now work with a student who took notes on one of the other types of love. Using your notes only, give an oral summary of the type of love that you took notes on.

D With your partner, make up three questions about the types of love that you took notes on.

3 Using quotations Ⓦ Ⓡ

As you read, identify some sentences or phrases that you might want to use in an assignment on the topic of the reading. Write them out carefully, making sure that you don't change any words by mistake. Also, write down next to the sentence or phrase the full name of the author of the reading and the title of the work from which the quotation comes.

A Review the information on Using Quotations on page 188. Note that this reading, "Types of Love," comes from the following source:

The Interpersonal Communication Book, by Joseph A. DeVito

B For each type of love in the text, find a sentence or phrase that you might use if you were writing about that type of love. For each type of love, write one or two sentences in which you include your chosen quotation. Remember to include the following:

- The author
- The source
- The exact wording
- The correct punctuation

C Show your sentences to a partner. Check each other's work for correct use of quotations.

4 Thinking about the topic Ⓡ

A It is possible that you may think that each type of love described in the reading has some negative qualities. Imagine, therefore, that you are a love chef. Your assignment is to cook up the perfect lover. Your ingredients are the six different types of love. What percentage of each type would you include in your recipe?

Eros   ___ %
Ludus   ___ %
Storge   ___ %
Mania   ___ %
Pragma   ___ %
Agape   ___ %

B Compare your percentages in a group and say why you created the recipe you did.

Predicting ®

In this text, you will read about the results of a survey of more than 1,000 American male and female college students ages 18 to 24. The students were asked about the romantic experiences that they had had so far in their lives.

A Work with a partner and predict the results for men and for women. Write your predictions in the chart.

	Average for Men	Average for Women
1. How many times have you been infatuated?		
2. How old were you when you were first infatuated?		
3. How many times have you fallen in love?		
4. How old were you when you first fell in love?		

B Compare predictions with another pair of students. In this new group of four students, tell each other how you would have answered these same questions if you had been asked for this information.

C Other research findings are given in this reading. Check (✓) the statements you think will be true according to this research.

☐ 1. Men score higher than women on ludic love (see page 197 for the definition of *ludic love*).

☐ 2. Men more often marry for love than women.

☐ 3. Men believe in love at first sight more than women.

☐ 4. Compared with women, men more often cause the breakup of a relationship because of finding another partner.

D Compare your answers with a partner's.

Reading 3

GENDER DIFFERENCES IN LOVING

In the United States, the differences between men and women in love are considered great. In poetry, novels, and the mass media, women and men are depicted as acting very differently when falling in love, being in love, and ending a love relationship. Women are
5 portrayed as emotional, men as logical. Women are supposed to love intensely; men are supposed to love with detachment.

In fact, women and men seem to experience love to a similar degree, and research continues to find great similarities between men's and women's conceptions of love. However, women indicate greater
10 love than men do for their same-sex friends. This may reflect a real difference between the sexes, or it may be a function of the greater social restrictions on men. A man is not supposed to admit his love for another man. Women are permitted greater freedom to communicate their love for other women.

15 Men and women also differ in the types of love they prefer. For example, men score higher on erotic and ludic love, whereas women score higher on manic, pragmatic, and storgic love.

Romantic experiences and attitudes

In an attempt to investigate women's and men's number of romantic experiences and the ages at which these occur, sociologist
20 William Kephart surveyed over 1,000 college students from 18 to 24 years of age. The women indicated that they had been infatuated more times than the men. The median number of times infatuated for the women was 5.6, and for the men, 4.5, For love relationships, there is greater similarity. The median number of times in love for
25 these same women was 1.3, and for the men, 1.1. Kephart predicted that women would have had their first romantic experience earlier than men and found this to be true. The median age at first infatuation for women was 13, and for men 13.6; the median age at first time in love for women was 17.1, and for men, 17.6.

30 Much research finds that men place more emphasis on romance than women. For example, college students from 11 different countries were asked the question "If a man (woman) had all the other qualities desired, would you marry this person if you were not in love with him (her)?" (See Figure 8.1 for results for both genders by country.)
35 Researchers found that a significantly higher percentage of men than women responded No, which seems to indicate that the men were more concerned with love and romance. Similarly, when men and women were surveyed concerning their view on love – whether basically realistic or basically romantic – it was found that married
40 women had a more realistic (less romantic) conception of love than did married men.

Fig. 8.1 Responses in 11 countries to the question "If a man (woman) had all the other qualities desired, would you marry this person if you were not in love with him (her)?"

Country	Percent Yes	Percent No	Percent Undecided
Japan	2.3	62.0	35.7
United States	3.5	85.9	10.6
Brazil	4.3	85.7	10.0
Australia	4.8	80.0	15.2
Hong Kong	5.8	77.6	16.7
England	7.3	83.6	9.1
Mexico	10.2	80.5	9.3
Philippines	11.4	63.6	25.0
Thailand	18.8	33.8	47.5
India	49.0	24.0	26.9
Pakistan	50.4	39.1	10.4

Source: LeVine, Sato, Hashimoto, & Verma

Additional research also supports the view that men are more romantic. For example, in an article describing their research into the romantic beliefs of men and women, Sprecher and Metts conclude,
45 "Men are more likely than women to believe in love at first sight, in love as the basis for marriage and for overcoming obstacles, and to believe that their partner and relationship will be perfect." This difference seems to increase as the romantic relationship develops – men become more romantic and women become less
50 romantic.

Romantic breakups

One further gender difference may be noted, and that is the difference between men and women in the reason for breaking up a relationship. Popular myth would have us believe that most love affairs break up as a result of the man's outside affair. But the research does not
55 support this. When surveyed as to the reason for breaking up, only 15 percent of the men indicated that it was their interest in another partner, whereas 32 percent of women noted this as a cause of the breakup. These findings are consistent with their partners' perceptions as well: 30 percent of the men (but only 15 percent of the women)
60 noted that their partner's interest in another person was the reason for the breakup.

In their reactions to broken romantic affairs, women and men exhibit similarities and differences. For example, the tendency for women and men to recall only pleasant memories and to revisit
65 places with past associations was about equal. However, men engaged in more dreaming about the lost partner and in more daydreaming generally as a reaction to the breakup than did women.

Research shows that women more often cause the breakup of a relationship, although myth might have us believe the opposite.

1 Reading for details ®

Test your understanding of this text by reading each statement in the table and placing a check (✓) in the appropriate column(s) depending on whether the statement is true for men or women or both.

	Men	Women
1. They are said to love more intensely.		
2. They show more love for same-sex friends.		
3. They have more infatuations.		
4. Between the ages of 18 and 24, the average number of times in love is less than two.		
5. The median age at first infatuation is between 13 and 14.		
6. The median age at first time in love is between 17 and 18.		
7. More say they would not marry someone if they were not in love with him or her.		
8. They more often cause the breakup of a relationship by becoming interested in another partner.		
9. They tend to remember only pleasant things after a breakup.		
10. After a breakup, they tend to daydream more about the lost partner.		

2 *Similar* and *Different* Ⓥ

When learning new forms of words that you are already familiar with, make sure you notice what words they collocate with and what grammatical structures they tend to occur in.

Not surprisingly, in a text that discusses how men and women are similar and different in the way they love, the words *similar* and *different* occur. However, since writers vary their language, sometimes they may use the noun, verb, adjective or adverb form of these words.

A Fill in the chart with the five missing word forms of *similar* and *different* (there is no verb form for *similar*).

Adjective	Noun	Verb	Adverb
similar			
different			

B All seven words appear in this reading. Find them all and circle them.

C These words collocate with certain other words and structures. Fill in the sentences with the words from the chart. The words in bold are the collocating words that you should notice as you complete the sentences.

1. Men and women **are** _____ **to** each other in the way they love.

2. Men and women **are** _____ **from** each other in the way they love.

3. There is **one major** _____ **in the way that** men and women love.

4. There is a **great** _____ **in the way** men and women love. They **both** . . .

5. There is a **great** _____ **in the way** men and women love. Men . . . , **but** women . . .

6. Men and women _____ **in how** they love.

7. There **is no real** _____ **in** the way men and women love.

8. Often men and women **act** _____ . Men . . . , **but** women . . .

9. Often men and women **behave** _____ . **Both** . . .

10. One **significant** _____ **between** men and women is . . .

D Use six different collocations and structures from the sentences above to make six true sentences about men, women, and love, according to the information in the reading. Use hedging language if necessary.

3 The passive voice Ⓦ

> The passive voice is used very often when the actual subject, or doer, of the action is unknown or unimportant.

A Look at these excerpts from the reading, which contain passive verbs. Go back to the text and work out who the "unknown" and "unspoken" agents, or doers, of these verbs are.

1. . . . the differences between men and women in love are considered great. (Lines 1–2)

2. . . . women and men are depicted as acting very differently . . . (Lines 2–3)

3. Women are portrayed as emotional, men as logical. (Lines 4–5)

4. . . . college students from 11 different countries were asked . . . (Lines 31–32)

5. . . . it was found that . . . (Line 39)

6. One further gender difference may be noted, . . . (Line 51)

B In Paragraph 4, we are told who the researcher who conducted the survey was. Summarize Paragraph 4 without mentioning William Kephart's name and use the passive to complete the summary below.

Over 1,000 students _____ . It _____ that both men and women had been infatuated and in love about the same number of times. Also, it _____ that women would start to have "romantic experiences" at a younger age than men. This _____ to be true.

4 Thinking critically ®

A In this text, a number of commonly held beliefs about men and women and love are explored. According to the text, research shows that some of these beliefs seem to be false and some seem to be true. Find examples of each in the text.

B Notice that the writer uses hedging language when discussing whether a commonly held belief is true. This means that there is room for doubt. Does your personal experience tend to make you believe that the beliefs that are shown to probably be false really are false? Explain.

C The research in Figure 8.1 was conducted in 1994. Do you think that the same results would be found in these countries today? Give reasons for your answer about countries in the chart that you know about, or about your own country.

Chapter 8 Academic Vocabulary Review

The following are some of the words that appear in Chapter 8. They all come from the Academic Word List, a list of words that researchers have discovered occur frequently in many different types of academic texts. If you can learn these words, it should help you when you have a reading in almost any academic discipline. For a complete list of all the Academic Word List words in this chapter and in all the other readings in this book, see the Appendix on pages 213–214.

Reading 1 Attraction Theory	Reading 2 Types of Love	Reading 3 Gender Differences in Loving
attributes (n) construct (v) dominant justify principle reinforcement	commitment compatibility exclusion potential (adj) unattainable unique	conception consistent exhibit (v) investigate logical survey (v)

Complete the following sentences with words from the lists above.

1. Why is it that unfortunately one so often falls in love with someone who is _____ ?

2. What _____ are you looking for in the perfect partner?

3. The researcher wants to _____ whether people are attracted to people who are more or less the same height.

4. It was not a difficult test design to _____ .

5. Every human being is surely _____ .

6. Everyone has their own _____ of what fidelity truly means.

7. All my friends _____ similar characteristics.

8. Maybe Jessica likes Tony as a friend, but I don't think she sees him as a _____ husband.

9. _____ is so important in a relationship. You don't have to have the same personality, but you have to like doing the same sorts of things together.

10. I live by one important _____ : Family comes first.

11. It is important to be _____ in a relationship. Nobody likes someone who is warm and friendly one moment and then cold and distant the next.

12. I think it is going to be difficult for you to _____ your behavior. I just don't understand why you did that.

Practicing Academic Writing

In Unit 4, you have learned about different types of friendship and love. You have learned about how people meet, what attracts people to each other, and how relationships develop. Use this information to write an essay on the topic below.

AN ANALYSIS OF INTERPERSONAL RELATIONSHIPS

Write an essay in which you analyze one or two of your personal relationships. Write on two or more of the following topics:

- The stages the relationships went through
- The reasons you were attracted
- The needs the relationships served
- The role, if any, that technology played in your relationships

Use quotations from the readings to point to similarities and differences between your relationship experiences and the concepts described in the readings.

PREPARING TO WRITE

1 Gathering ideas

When you are given an essay assignment, you need to gather ideas. Later you can organize them so that you can see how the ideas can come together in an essay that has a thesis and supporting details.

Throughout this book, you have used different techniques for gathering ideas before you write: Making Lists (page 51) and Freewriting (page 105). In addition, you have reread parts of units and found passages to paraphrase and summarize. For this assignment, you will also need to reread the texts in the unit and look for quotations that you might include in your writing.

A Make a list of three relationships that you have had and complete the chart.

Name of Friend	How, Where, and What Happened When You Met	Things You Do Together	Reasons You Get Along	Uses of Communications Technology with Friend

B Choose one of the friends in your chart. Review your notes and freewrite about that person for five minutes. When you have finished, read through your freewriting and find two or three ideas and phrases that you might be able to use in your essay.

C Read the reading in this unit that is on the topics in the essay assignment you are going to write about and summarize it in a brief paragraph.

D Choose a couple of key passages in one of the readings related to the topics in the essay assignment you are going to write about and paraphrase them.

E Find a few quotations from one or more readings in the unit that you think you could include in your essay. Write them on note cards.

F Remember, the author of these readings is Joseph A. DeVito and the readings come from a book called *The Interpersonal Communications Book*. Include that information on the note cards. Use quotation marks around the quotations to remind yourself that these are the exact words from the reading.

2 Journal writing

Very often an academic essay assignment will require that you draw from your personal experience. The purpose of such assignments is to see whether you have understood the theoretical concepts in your reading and whether you can apply them to your own experience. It also ensures that your essay will be fresh and original, since what you have to say will be based on your personal experience and it will therefore be unique. By keeping journal entries, in which you record your personal responses to readings, you will have a starting point for writing on such assignments.

A The journal writing that you have done while studying this unit will also give you ideas for your essay. Review the journal writing that you did for Task 5 on page 174, in which you responded to the reading "What Is Friendship?" You wrote about the needs friends serve in our lives and the stages in a relationship. See if there are ideas in this journal entry that you could use in your essay. Make notes.

B Review the journal writing that you did for Task 5 on page 195, in which you responded to the reading "Attraction Theory." See if there are any ideas in this journal entry that you could use in your essay. Make notes.

C Reread "The Internet and Relationships" on pages 181–182 and "Gender Differences in Loving" on pages 203–204. Decide which of the two readings most closely relates to the topic of the essay you are going to write. Then write a journal entry in which you make a personal response to that reading.

NOW WRITE

Finding a focus

Before you start writing an academic essay, you have to find a controlling idea – your thesis. All academic essay writing involves presenting an idea that you have to prove or defend with supporting facts and arguments. Not all essay assignments, however, clearly present you with a direction for your writing. It is up to you to interpret the essay assignment and find an interesting point of view to put forward as your thesis.

The Unit 4 writing assignment does not present you with a clear direction for your essay. You have many possible topics to write about and it is up to you to take one or two of those topics and find a controlling idea.

A Read the following students' thesis statements for the writing assignment for this unit. Discuss with a partner which ones you think will and will not lead to a well-focused academic essay with an interesting point of view.

1. In this essay, I will describe a friendship that I had for many years which came to an end last summer.
2. My friendship with X clearly demonstrates that we can be attracted to people who are very different from us and who serve, as DeVito writes, a "stimulation" need.
3. The Internet has changed the way people form and maintain their relationships.
4. DeVito says that we are attracted to people in one of six different ways and that friendship serves one of five different needs.

B Look back at your notes and all the ideas that you gathered in Preparing to Write. Write a controlling idea that can be used in your introduction to provide a focus for your essay.

C Organize your notes and create a brief outline of your essay.

Conclusions

An academic essay requires a closing paragraph or paragraphs that remind your reader of your main ideas and give the reader something to reflect on when they have finished reading. It is, not surprisingly, the last thing that you write because it provides a summary and a reflection of your ideas.

D Write your first draft and include a conclusion that reviews the main idea of your essay and gives the reader something to think about when they have finished reading.

AFTER YOU WRITE

A Read through your essay or ask a friend to read through it. You or your friend should look for things that are unclear, confusing, or unconvincing. Then revise your essay. Answer the following questions to check whether your essay has the parts of a standard academic essay. Make changes in your second draft if it doesn't.

1. *Did you include a thesis statement in your introductory paragraph?*
Check to see that you have a thesis statement that prepares the reader for the body of the essay.

2. *Did you include topic sentences with your body paragraphs?*
Check your body paragraphs to see if you have written a general opening statement that prepares the reader for your ideas in the rest of the paragraph.

3. *Did you support your topic sentences well?*
Check to see if you have enough details to make the reader feel that your topic sentences are convincing. If not, add more details.

4. *Did you write a conclusion to your essay?*
Check to see if you wrote a conclusion that reminds the reader of your thesis.

B Read through your essay to edit it.

1. Look back at Task 3, Efficient Sentence Structure, on page 172. Have you tried to write some sentences in which you "pack" a lot of information into one sentence by using a string of adjectives, verb phrases, or noun phrases? Find places where you might use such sentence structures in your essay.

2. When analyzing relationships in your essay, have you written about similarities and differences? Look back at Task 2, *Similar* and *Different*, on page 205. See if you have used a variety of forms of these words in your writing. If not, try to include some in your writing.

3. Remember that prepositions can be tricky. Look back at Task 4, Prepositions, on page 195. Check the use of prepositions in your essay. If you are unsure about which preposition to use with a particular word, use a dictionary to check.

4. In this essay, you were required to include quotations. Check that you have followed the guidelines on page 188 and punctuated your essay properly.

5. Read through your essay now for possible spelling mistakes, punctuation errors, subject-verb agreement errors, and incorrect use of the past tense and articles. Make corrections whenever you find errors.

Appendix

Academic Word List vocabulary

abnormally
abstractly
access
accompany
accuracy
accurate
achieve
achievement
acknowledge
adapt
adaptation
adjust
adjustment
adult
adulthood
affect
aid
alter
alternatively
ambiguity
analysis
analyze
annually
anticipated
apparent
apparently
appreciate
appreciation
approach
approachable
appropriate
approximately
arbitrary
area
aspect
assembly
assign
assist
assume
attain
attitude
attribute
authority
automatically

aware
awareness
beneficial
benefit
bulk
capable
capacity
categorize
challenge
channel
chapter
chart
chemical
circumstance
cite
civil
clarify
classic
coherent
collapse
comment
commit
commitment
communicate
communication
community
compatibility
compensate
compensation
complex
complexity
concentrate
concept
conception
conclude
conclusion
conduct
conference
confirm
conflict
conformity
consequence
consequently
considerable

considerably
consistent
consistently
constant
constantly
construct
construction
consult
consumption
contact
context
contradiction
contradictory
contrast
contribute
convince
coordinating
correspond
couple
create
cultural
culturally
culture
data
decade
decline
definable
define
definition
demonstrate
denial
depress
depression
deriving
despite
detect
devote
diminish
display
document
dominance
dominant
dominate
drama

dramatic
duration
dynamic
element
eliminate
emerge
emphasis
emphasize
enable
encounter
energetic
energy
enforcement
enhance
environment
establish
estimate
evaluate
eventually
evidence
evident
exceed
exclusion
exclusive
exhibit
expand
expert
expose
factor
final
finally
financial
flexible
focus
foundation
framework
function
fundamental
furthermore
gender
generate
generation
globe
goal

grade
grant
hence
hypothesis
identify
ignore
illustrate
image
impact
implement
impose
inadequacy
inappropriate
income
index
indicate
indicative
individual
induce
initial
initiated
injure
insert
instance
institute
instructor
integrate
intelligence
intelligent
intense
intensify
intensity
interact
interaction
intermediate
interpret
investigate
involve
involvement
irrational
irrelevant
isolation
issue
item

213

Academic Word List vocabulary *continued*

job
journal
justify
label
legal
likewise
link
logic
logical
maintain
major
majority
manipulation
maturation
mature
maturity
maximize
maximum
mechanism
media
medical
mental
migrate
minimize
minor
modification
modify
monitor
mutual
mutually
negative
networking
network
neutral
neutralize
normal
normally

obvious
occupation
occur
odds
oriented
outcome
overall
panel
parallel
participant
passive
perceive
percent
percentage
perception
period
perspective
phase
phenomena
philosophy
physical
plus
positive
potential
predict
predictable
predominant
presume
previous
primary
principle
process
professional
project
promotion
proportion
prospective

psychological
psychologist
psychology
publish
pursue
randomly
range
react
reaction
reassess
region
regulate
regulation
regulator
reinforce
reinforcement
reject
relax
relaxation
release
reliable
rely
relocation
reluctant
remove
require
research
researcher
resolution
resolve
resource
respond
response
responsiveness
restriction
retain
reveal

reverse
role
schedule
section
secure
security
seek
select
series
sex
sexual
sexuality
shift
significant
signify
similar
similarity
similarly
simulate
site
somewhat
sought
specific
specify
stability
stable
status
strategy
stress
stressful
style
substitute
summarize
survey
survival
survive
sustain

target
task
technical
technique
theorist
theory
thereby
trace
traditional
traditionally
transition
trend
trigger
ultimate
unattainable
undergo
underlie
undertake
underwent
uninvolved
unique
utility
variable
variation
vary
vehicle
via
violate
virtual
virtually
visibly
visual
volume
voluntary
whereas
widespread

Skills index

Credits

Text Credits

Pages 5–6, 12–14, 19–21, 30–32, 36–38. *Psychology: Being Human: Brief/Update* by Zick Rubin and Elton B. McNeil, 1987, pp. 312–314, 316–317, 319–323, 331.

Pages 36–38, 44–46, 70–74, 91–92, 97–99. *Psychology: Eighth Edition* in Modules by David G. Myers © 2007 Worth Publishers, New York, pp. 166, 171, 174, 181, 183–185, 569–570, 574–576, 579–580, 582–584.

Pages 59–60, 64–65, 70–74, 83–86, 91–92, 97–99. *Fundamentals of Psychology* by Josh R. Gerow, Thomas Brothern, and Jerry D. Newell © 1989 HarperCollins Publishers Inc., pp. 256–274

Pages 83–86. *Emerging Adulthood: The Winding Road from Late Teens Through the Twenties* by Jeffrey Jensen Arnett © 2004 Oxford University Press.

Pages 113–115, 121–123, 128–130, 138–139, 144–145, 160–162, 167–170, 191–192, 197–199, 203–204. *The Interpersonal Communication Book,* 12th Edition by Joseph DeVito © 2009 Pearson Education Inc., pp. 129–138, 142–143, 153–155, 218–219, 240, 247–250, 252–255, 257–258.

Pages 176–177, 203–204. *The Interpersonal Communication Book,* 7th Edition by Joseph DeVito © 1995 HarperCollins Publishers Inc., pp. 321, 323, 436.

Pages 181–182. *Psychology Applied to Modern Life: Adjustment in the 21st Century,* 9th Edition by Weiten, Lloyd, Dunn, and Hammer, © 2009 Cengage Learning, pp. 238–240.

Illustration Credits

Page 10: Copyright © 1970, Elsevier

Pages 13, 111, 182: Rob Schuster

Page 64: from "Standards from Birth to Maturity for Height, Weight, Height Velocity, and Weight Velocity: British Children, 1965" in Archives of Diseases in Childhood, 41, October 1966, by J.M. Tanner et. al. Copyright ©1966, BMJ Publishing Group Ltd and the Royal College of Paediatrics and Child Health

Page 194: Carly Monardo

Photography Credits

1 ©Studio Peter Frank/Digital Vision/Getty Images; 5 ©Raoul Minsart/Radius Images/Getty Images; 6 ©Al Bello/Getty Images; 14 ©Tom Grill/Photographer's Choice RF/Getty Images; 19 ©Carol Kohen/Cultura/Newscom; 20 ©AP Photo/Suzanne Plunkett; 21 ©George Doyle/Stockbyte/Getty Images; 30 ©Neil Guegan/Age Fotostock; 32 *(left to right)* ©Marili Forastieri/Photodisc/Getty Images; ©Radius Images/Alamy; 36 ©Ian Hooton/Science Photo Library/Getty Images; 38 ©European Community/Getty Images; 42 *(top to bottom)* ©Bamboosil/Age Fotostock; ©Neil Guegan/Age Fotostock; 46 ©RK Studio/Blend Images/Getty Images; 55 ©FoodPix/Jupiterimages/Getty Images; 59 *(top to bottom)* ©Hemera Technologies/AbleStock.com/Thinkstock; ©Jupiterimages/FoodPix/Getty Images; 60 ©Nancy Ney/Digital Vision/Getty Images; 65 ©ColorBlind Images/Iconica/Getty Images; 68 ©Alan Antiporda/Flickr/Getty Images; 70 ©Ted Horowitz/Age Fotostock; 71 ©Ted Streshinsky/Time Life Pictures/Getty Images; 72 ©iStockphoto/Thinkstock; 73 ©Tetra Images/Getty Images; 74 ©DreamPictures/Blend Images; 83 ©Eric Audras/PhotoAlto/Alamy; 85 ©Rubberball/Getty Images; 86 ©LWA/Dann Tardif/Blend Images/Getty Images; 89 ©Jamie Grill/JGI/Blend Images/Getty Images; 91 ©Comstock Images/Getty Images; 99 ©AP Photo/Patrick Gardin; 109 ©Ingram Publishing/Thinkstock; 113 *(top to bottom)* ©1809056 Ontario Ltd./Shutterstock; ©Yuri Arcurs/Alamy; 115 ©iStockphoto/Thinkstock; 122 ©Özgür Donmaz/iStockphoto; 123 ©Image Source/Getty Images; 128 ©Sam Edwards/OJO Images/Getty Images; 129 ©Ian Hooton/Science Photo Library/Alamy; 130 ©Veronique Beranger/Photographer's Choice/Getty Images; 133 ©BananaStock/Punchstock; 138 ©Creatas/Thinkstock; 139 ©DAJ/Getty Images; 142 ©Stuart O'Sullivan/The Image Bank/Getty Images; 143 *(left to right)* ©AP Photo/Markus Schreiber; ©Floresco Productions/OJO Images/Getty Images; ©Dave & Les Jacobs/Blend Images/Getty Images; ©John Lund/Marc Romanelli/Blend Images/Getty Images; 144 ©Nico Kai/Iconica/Getty Images; 145 ©Ryan McVay/The Image Bank/Getty Images; 149 ©Image Source/Getty Images; 150 *(left to right)* ©Hemera/Thinkstock; ©iStockphoto/Thinkstock; ©Hemera/Thinkstock; ©Zoonar/Thinkstock; 151 ©STOCK4B-RF/Getty Images; 153 ©ArabianEye/Getty Images; 163 ©Mallory Samson/Workbook Stock/Getty Images; 167 ©PunchStock/Science Photo Library; 168 ©moodboard/The Agency Collection/Getty Images; 169 ©Kablonk/Golden Pixels LLC/Alamy; 174 ©Jamie Grill/JGI/Blend Images/Getty Images 177 ©StockbrokerXtra/Age Fotostock; 179 ©Bambu Productions/Iconica/Getty Images; 181 ©A.CollectionRF/Getty Images Images; 191 ©GM Visuals/Blend Images/Getty Images; 192 ©Andrew H. Walker/Getty Images; 196 ©Multi-bits/The Image Bank/Getty Images; 198 ©Fotosearch/Getty Images; 199 ©Tetra Images/Alamy; 203 ©Radius Images/PunchStock; 204 ©Jamie Grill/Iconica/Getty Images